Essential Italian Grammar

By
OLGA RAGUSA
Professor of Italian
Columbia University
and
The Editorial Staff of
DOVER PUBLICATIONS, INC.

DOVER PUBLICATIONS, INC.
NEW YORK, NEW YORK

Essential Italian Grammar is a new work, first published by
Dover Publications, Inc., in 1963.

International Standard Book Number: 0-486-20779-X
Library of Congress Catalog Card Number: 63-2911

Manufactured in the United States of America
Dover Publications, Inc.
180 Varick Street
New York, N. Y. 10014

Table of Contents

3

Introduction

Essential Italian Grammar is based on the assumption that you plan to spend a limited number of hours studying Italian grammar and that your objective is simple everyday communication. This book is not a condensed outline of all aspects of Italian grammar. It is a series of hints to help you use more effectively and with greater versatility phrases and vocabulary that you have already learned.

How to Study Essential Italian Grammar

If you have already studied Italian in a conventional manner, you can use this book as a refresher by glancing through all of it first and then selecting those areas on which you wish to concentrate.

If you have never studied Italian grammar, then the following suggestions will be helpful:

1. Master several hundred useful phrases and expressions such as you will find in any good phrase book or in the *Listen & Learn Italian* course. You will understand the suggestions contained in *Essential Italian Grammar* more easily after you have achieved this basic working knowledge of Italian. The purpose of this book is to enable you to gain greater fluency once you have learned phrases and expressions, not to teach you to construct sentences from rules and vocabulary.

2. Read through *Essential Italian Grammar* at least once in its entirety. Don't be concerned if anything is not immediately clear to you. What may appear discouragingly difficult at first will become easier as your studies progress. But the first reading is necessary to acquaint you with terms and concepts peculiar to Italian grammar. Learning what these terms and concepts are will help you to improve your comprehension of Italian and to use more freely the expressions you already know. As you use Italian and hear it spoken, many of its grammatical patterns will become familiar to you. *Essential Italian Grammar* helps you to discover these patterns so that you can use them.

3. Go back to this book periodically. Sections which seem difficult or of doubtful benefit at first, may prove extremely useful later.

4. For the most part, the book follows a logical order, taking up the major divisions of grammar in sequence. You will do best to follow this order. However, some students learn best when they study to answer an immediate question or need (e.g., how to form the comparative; how to conjugate the verb "to be," etc.). If you are one of these students, turn to the section that interests you. But read through the entire section, rather than just an isolated part. Individual remarks, taken out of context, are easily misunderstood.

5. Examples are given for every rule. It is helpful to memorize these examples. If you learn every example in *Essential Italian Grammar*, together with its literal translation, you will have encountered the basic difficulties of Italian and studied models for their solution.

6. You cannot study Italian systematically without an understanding of its grammar, and the use and understanding of grammatical terms is as essential as a knowledge of certain mechanical terms when you learn to drive a car. If your knowledge of grammatical terms is weak, read the Glossary of Grammatical Terms (p. 94) and refer to it whenever necessary.

In every language there are many ways to express the same thought. Some constructions are simple, others more difficult. During your first experiments in communication, use a simple construction. Throughout *Essential Italian Grammar* you will find suggestions on how to avoid complicated constructions in favor of simpler ones. You may ultimately wish to master a more sophisticated way of expressing yourself. Be satisfied at first with the simplest.

As you begin to speak Italian, you will become aware of the areas in which you need the most help in grammar. If you have no one with whom to speak, speak mentally to yourself. In the course of a day see how many of the simple thoughts you've expressed in English you are able to turn into Italian. This kind of experimental self-testing will give direction to your study of grammar. Remember that you are studying this course in Italian not to pass an examination or to receive a certificate, but to communicate with others on a simple but useful level. *Essential Italian Grammar* is not the equivalent of a formal course of study at a university. Although it could serve as a supplement to such a course, its primary aim is to help the adult study on his own. Indeed, no self-study or academic course or series of courses is ever ideally suited to all students. You must rely on and be guided by your own rate of learning and your own requirements and interests. *Essential Italian Grammar* makes self-study easier.

If this or any other grammar tends to inhibit you in speaking Italian or in using what you have learned through phrase books, conversation courses, or the *Listen & Learn* records, curtail your study of grammar until you feel it will really assist rather than hinder your speaking. Your objective is speaking, and you *can* learn to speak a language without learning its grammar. But because of its systematic approach, grammar is a short-cut to language learning for those who feel at home with it. The fundamental purpose of *Essential Italian Grammar* is to help you by eliminating hit-or-miss memorization.

Suggestions for Vocabulary Building

1. Study words and word lists that answer real and preferably immediate personal needs. If you are planning to travel in the near future, your motivation and orientation is clear cut and *Listen & Learn Italian* or a good travel phrase book will provide you with the material you need. But select from this material that specifically applies to your case. For instance, if you don't plan to motor, don't spend time studying the parts of the car. If you like foreign foods, study the supplementary Italian food list in *Listen & Learn Italian*. Even if you do not plan to travel in the near future, you will probably learn more quickly by imagining a travel situation.

2. Memorize by association. Phrase books and *Listen & Learn Italian* usually give associated word lists. If you use a dictionary, don't memorize words haphazardly but choose words which are related and belong to the same family.

3. Study the specialized vocabulary of your profession, business, or hobby. If you are interested in real estate, learn the terms associated with property, buying, selling, leasing, etc. If you are interested in mathematics, acquire a vocabulary in this science. Many of these specialized words can be used in other areas too. You may not find specialized vocabularies in ordinary phrase books, but a good dictionary will help you to make up a list for your own use.

Similarities between English and Italian Vocabulary

It will help you to expand your Italian vocabulary if you remember that many Italian words are similar in appearance and meaning to English words. Notice: *la radio* (the radio), *la professione* (the profession), *la medicina* (the medicine), *il telefono* (the telephone), *il teatro* (the theater), *politico* (political).

Here are some common differences in spelling between English and Italian:

English *k* or *ck* =	Italian *c* or *cc*	par*k*—par*c*o; sa*ck*—sa*cc*o
„ *ph*	„ *f*	*ph*rase—*f*rase;
		tele*ph*one—tele*f*ono
„ *x*	„ *s* or *ss*	fi*x*ed—fi*ss*o;
		e*x*ercise—e*s*ercizio
„ *th*	„ *t*	*th*eater—*t*eatro
„ *c*	„ *z* or *zz*	for*c*e—for*z*a; ra*c*e—ra*zz*a
„ *y*	„ *i*	st*y*le—st*i*le
„ *ou*	„ *o*	c*ou*rt—c*o*rte
„ *tion*	„ *zione*	conversa*tion*—conversa*zione*
„ *ous*	„ *oso*	fam*ous*—fam*oso*

Study this list of words, observing the differences between English and Italian:

ENGLISH	ITALIAN
automobile	automobile
hotel	hotel
area	area
gas	gas
idea	idea
radio	radio
color	colore
annual	annuale
commercial	commerciale
special	speciale

list	lista
problem	problema
person	persona
cost	costo
moment	momento

cause	causa
figure	figura
medicine	medicina
rose	rosa
minute	minuto
use	uso
tube	tubo

generous	generoso
delicious	delizioso
famous	famoso
precious	prezioso

philosophy	filosofia
geography	geografia
history	storia

nation	nazione
action	azione
collection	collezione

Word Order

Word order in Italian is frequently the same as in English. This, added to the similarities between many English and Italian words, often makes it easy to understand an Italian sentence even with a minimum knowledge of grammar. Compare the following sentences in Italian and in English:

Roma è la capitale d'Italia.
Rome is the capital of Italy.

I turisti visitano musei, teatri e monumenti.
The tourists visit museums, theaters, and monuments.

How to Form Questions

You can turn a simple statement into a question in one of the following three ways:

1. Leave the sentence as it is and simply add a question mark at the end. When speaking, raise your voice at the end of the sentence. This is often done in English too.

Mio padre è arrivato?
My father has arrived?

Lei parla inglese?
You speak English?

2. Invert the normal order of subject and predicate* and place the predicate before the subject.

È arrivato mio padre?
[Has arrived my father?]
Has my father arrived?

Parla inglese Lei?
[Speak English you?]
Do† you speak English?

È la capitale d'Italia Roma?
[Is the capital of Italy Rome?]
Is Rome the capital of Italy?

3. Leave the sentence as it is and simply add *non è vero?* [not is true?] at the end. *Non è vero?* is the Italian equivalent of such English phrases as "isn't it?" "don't you?" "aren't you?" etc.

Suo padre parla inglese, *non è vero?*
Your father speaks English, *doesn't he?*

* If you are not familiar with the terms and concepts used in grammar, turn now to the Glossary of Grammatical Terms at the end of the book.
† The verb "to do"—used in English questions such as "*Do* you want some coffee?"— is not used in this way in Italian.

Il primo capitolo è lungo, *non è vero?*
The first chapter is long, *isn't it?*

Interrogative Words

Most questions, in Italian as in English, begin with a question word such as "when?" "where?" "who?" Study the following list carefully:

Come	How	*Come* si dice in italiano?
		[How itself (it) says in Italian?]
		How do you say (this) in Italian?
Quando	When	*Quando* parte l'ultimo treno?
		[When leaves the last train?]
		When does the last train leave?
Dove	Where	*Dove* siamo?
		[Where we are?]
		Where are we?
Chi	Who	*Chi* viene con noi?
		Who comes with us?
Di chi	Whose	*Di chi* è questa valigia?
		[Of whom is this suitcase?]
		Whose suitcase is this?
Quale	Which	*Quale* preferisce Lei?
		[Which prefer you?]
		Which do you prefer?
Che, Che cosa	What	*Che* desidera? *Che cosa* desidera?
		[What you wish? What thing you wish?]
		What do you wish?
Perchè	Why	*Perchè* viaggia Lei?
		[Why travel you?]
		Why do you travel?

| *Quanto* | How much | *Quanto* costa?
[How much costs?]
How much does it cost? |
| *Quanti* | How many | *Quanti* sono venuti?
[How many are come?]
How many have come? |

Nouns and Articles

Gender of Italian Nouns

All Italian nouns are either masculine or feminine. In general, nouns denoting male persons or animals are masculine, and nouns denoting female persons or animals are feminine. This rule, however, cannot be used as a guide for identifying the gender of the countless nouns which do not denote persons or animals. The best way to learn the gender of nouns is to memorize the definite article together with the noun.

The Definite Article

In Italian, the definite article agrees in gender and number with the noun it accompanies. English is simpler in this respect, for the same form, "the," is used for all nouns, singular or plural. The forms of the definite article in Italian are:

MASC. SING.	MASC. PL.
il	*i*
lo	*gli*
l'	*gl'*

FEM. SING.	FEM. PL.
la	*le*
l'	*le*

Observations on the definite article:

Il and *i*, *la*, and *le* are the most common forms of the definite article.

Lo and *gli* are used before masculine nouns beginning with *z*, or with *s* followed by a consonant: *lo* zio (the uncle), *lo* sbaglio (the mistake).

Gli is also used before masculine plurals beginning with a vowel: *gli* anni (the years).

Gl' is used before masculine plurals beginning with *i*: *gl'*italiani (the Italians).

L' is used before singular nouns, masculine and feminine, beginning with a vowel: *l'*anno (the year), *l'*opera (the opera).

Study the following table carefully:

	SING.		PL.	
MASC.	*il*	*il* signore, the gentleman	*i*	*i* signori, the gentlemen
	lo	*lo* zio, the uncle	*gli*	*gli* zii, the uncles
		lo sbaglio, the mistake		*gli* sbagli, the mistakes
	l'	*l'*anno, the year		*gli* anni, the years
			gl'	*gl'*italiani, the Italians
FEM.	*la*	*la* signora, the lady	*le*	*le* signore, the ladies
	l'	*l'*italiana, the Italian woman		*le* italiane, the Italian women
				le entrate, the entrances

Plurals of Nouns

The majority of masculine nouns end in -*o* in the singular and change this -*o* to -*i* in the plural: il teatr*o* (the theater), i teatr*i* (the theaters).

The majority of feminine nouns end in -*a* in the singular and change this -*a* to -*e* in the plural: la donn*a* (the woman), le donn*e* (the women).

Nouns which end in -*e* in the singular may be either masculine or feminine. These nouns change the -*e* to -*i* in the plural: la madr*e* (the mother), le madr*i* (the mothers); il padr*e* (the father), i padr*i* (the fathers).

There are a number of masculine nouns which end in -*a* in the singular. They change the -*a* to -*i* in the plural: il poet*a* (the poet), i poet*i* (the poets).

	SING.	PL.	
feminine nouns ending in	-a	.........-e	la donna, le donne
masculine nouns ending in	-o		il libro, i libri
masculine nouns ending in	-a	.........-i	il poeta, i poeti
masculine nouns ending in	-e		il padre, i padri
feminine nouns ending in	-e		la madre, le madri

Irregularities in Noun Plurals

1. A number of masculine nouns ending in -o in the singular become feminine in the plural and have an irregular plural ending in -a. The most common of these nouns are:

SING.	PL.
l'uovo (the egg)	le uova (the eggs)
il braccio (the arm)	le braccia (the arms)
il dito (the finger)	le dita (the fingers)
il lenzuolo (the sheet)	le lenzuola (the sheets)
il paio (the pair)	le paia (the pairs)

2. Nouns ending in -io are of two kinds:

(a) When the *i* of -io is stressed, the -o is changed to -i:
lo zio (the uncle), gli zii (the uncles)

(b) When the *i* of -io is not stressed, it drops out before the -o is changed to -i:
il figlio (the son), i figli (the sons)

3.(a) Nouns ending in -co and -go may or may not insert an *h* before changing the -o to -i. There is no simple general rule for this.

SING.	PL.
il medico (the doctor)	i medici (the doctors)
l'amico (the friend)	gli amici (the friends)
il fuoco (the fire)	i fuochi (the fires)
il fisiologo (the physiologist)	i fisiologi (the physiologists)
il lago (the lake)	i laghi (the lakes)

(b) Nouns ending in *-ca* and *-ga* insert an *h* before changing the *-a* to *-e*.

l'ami*ca* (the friend)   le ami*che* (the friends)
la pag*a* (the salary)   le pag*he* (the salaries)

4. Nouns ending in an accented vowel do not change in the plural: la città (the city), le città (the cities).

5. *L'uomo* (the man) has an irregular plural, *gli uomini* (the men).

Noun Suffixes

A special feature of Italian nouns is that their meaning can be modified by the addition of suffixes. Thus *ragazzo* (boy) can become *ragazzino* or *ragazzetto* (little boy), *ragazzone* (big overgrown boy), and *ragazzaccio* (brat, nasty boy). *Casa* (house) can become *casetta* (little house), *libro* (book) can become *libriccino* (little book). The use of these and other suffixes is very frequent in idiomatic Italian and it is well for you to be aware of it, even if you do not make use of suffixes yourself.

Hints on the Identification of Gender

We have already said that the best way for you to remember the gender of a noun is to memorize the noun together with its article. There are, however, a few general rules which can help you in recognizing and remembering the gender of a noun.

1. You can recognize the gender of a noun by its ending.
   (a) Masculine nouns generally end in *-o*: *il figlio* (the son).
   (b) Feminine nouns generally end in *-a*: *la donna* (the woman).
   Exceptions: *la mano* (the hand), *il poeta* (the poet), *il programma* (the program), and a number of others.

2. The gender of a noun may be recognized by its meaning.

MASC. (a) The names of male persons and animals are almost always masculine: *il padre* (the father), *il leone* (the lion).

(b) The names of the months and of the days of the week (except Sunday) are masculine: *il settembre* (September), *il lunedì* (Monday).

(c) The names of mountains and lakes are masculine: *il Vesuvio* (Vesuvius), *il Garda* (Lake Garda).

FEM. (d) The names of female persons and animals are usually feminine: *la madre* (the mother), *la leonessa* (the lioness).

(e) Abstract nouns of quality ending in an accented syllable are feminine: *la libertà* (liberty), *la virtù* (virtue).

(f) Names of almost all fruits are feminine: *la pera* (the pear), *la mela* (the apple).

Masculine and Feminine Forms of the Same Noun

You can enlarge your vocabulary by observing the following changes in nouns:

(1) Changing the final vowel can make a masculine noun feminine:

Francesc*o* (Francis)—Francesc*a* (Frances)
figli*o* (son)—figli*a* (daughter)
sart*o* (tailor)—sart*a* (seamstress)
infermier*e* (male nurse)—infermier*a* (nurse)
padron*e* (boss, owner)—padron*a* (boss's wife, owner)

(2) Dropping the final vowel and adding a suffix can make a masculine noun feminine:

poeta (poet)—poet*essa* (poetess)
studente (student, masc.)—student*essa* (student, fem.)

(3) Some nouns refer to both male and female persons and adjust their gender accordingly:

il nipote (the nephew)—*la* nipote (the niece)
il cantante (the singer, masc.)—*la* cantante (the singer, fem.)

Common Prepositions and the Definite Article

The most common Italian prepositions when used together with the definite article are contracted as follows:

PREPOSITION	DEFINITE ARTICLE							
	SINGULAR				PLURAL			
	il	*lo*	*la*	*l'*	*i*	*gli*	*gl'*	*le*
a, to, at	al	allo	alla	all'	ai	agli	agl'	alle
da, from, by	dal	dallo	dalla	dall'	dai	dagli	dagl'	dalle
di, of	del	dello	della	dell'	dei	degli	degl'	delle
in, in	nel	nello	nella	nell'	nei	negli	negl'	nelle
su, on	sul	sullo	sulla	sull'	sui	sugli	sugl'	sulle
con, with	col	No contractions with other forms of the definite article.						
per, for	Does not contract at all.							

Determine first what the proper form of the definite article is and then use the contracted form that corresponds to it.

Non ci sono posti liberi *nella* sala da pranzo.
[Not there are places free *in the* room for dining.]
There are no empty places *in the* dining room.

Il prezzo *del* biglietto è seicento lire.
The price *of the* ticket is 600 Lire.

Cerco un regalo *per il* compleanno di mia figlia.
[I seek a gift *for the* birthday of my daughter.]
I am looking for a gift for my daughter's birthday.

Andremo *all'*opera *con gli* altri.
We shall go *to the* opera *with the* others.

The Indefinite Article

In English the indefinite article "a" becomes "an" when it

precedes a vowel. In Italian, the indefinite article agrees in gender with the noun it accompanies.

Study the following table:

MASC.	*un*	*un* signore (a gentleman); *un* attore (an actor)
	uno	*uno* zio (an uncle)
FEM.	*una*	*una* cugina (a (girl) cousin)
	un'	*un'*amica (a (girl) friend)

Observations on the indefinite article:

Un is the usual form of the indefinite article used before a masculine noun; *una* is the usual form used before a feminine noun.

Uno is used before masculine nouns beginning with *z*, or with *s* followed by a consonant: *uno* zero (a zero), *uno* sbaglio (a mistake).

Un' is used before all feminine nouns beginning with a vowel: *un'*italiana (an Italian woman).

The indefinite article has no plural. To express an indefinite plural ("some") use the preposition *di* with the definite article: *dei* ragazzi (some boys), *delle* donne (some women).

Adjectives

Agreement of Adjectives with Nouns

In Italian, adjectives agree in gender and number with the nouns they accompany. A masculine singular noun requires a masculine singular adjective, a feminine singular noun a feminine singular adjective, etc. In English, the use of adjectives is simpler because they are invariable: a *red* house, two *red* houses.

Forms of Adjectives

There are two kinds of adjectives in Italian: those which end in -*o* in the masculine singular, and those which end in -*e* in both the masculine and feminine singular.

1. Adjectives ending in -*o*:

	SING.	PL.
MASC.	italian*o* (Italian)	italian*i* (Italian)
	ross*o* (red)	ross*i* (red)
FEM.	italian*a* (Italian)	italian*e* (Italian)
	ross*a* (red)	ross*e* (red)

2. Adjectives ending in -*e*:

MASC.	ingles*e* (English)	ingles*i* (English)
	cortes*e* (polite)	cortes*i* (polite)
FEM.	ingles*e* (English)	ingles*i* (English)
	cortes*e* (polite)	cortes*i* (polite)

l'uomo italian*o*	the Italian man
gli uomini italian*i*	the Italian men
la donna italian*a*	the Italian woman
le donne italian*e*	the Italian women

25

l'uomo ingle*se*	the English man
la donna ingle*se*	the English woman
gli uomini ingle*si*	the English men
le donne ingle*si*	the English women

Observations on adjectives:

Adjectives like *italiano* have four different endings (italian*o*, italian*a*, italian*i*, italian*e*).

Adjectives like *cortese* have only two different endings (cortes*e*, cortes*i*).

Position of Adjectives

In Italian the adjective usually follows the noun:

una parola *cortese*, a *polite* word
un lenzuolo *bianco*, a *white* sheet
una lingua *difficile*, a *difficult* language
dei viaggi *lunghi*,* some *long* trips

A number of very common adjectives, however, often precede the noun in Italian, as in English:

bello, beautiful, handsome, fine	una *bella* ragazza (a *good-looking* girl)
buono, good	*buone* notizie (*good* news)
nuovo, new	un *nuovo* ristorante (a *new* restaurant)
vecchio, old	un *vecchio* amico (an *old* friend)
piccolo, small	un *piccolo* regalo (a *small* gift)
grande, big, large	una *grande* città (a *big* city)
lungo, long	una *lunga* strada (a *long* road)
breve, short	un *breve* soggiorno (a *short* stay)
giovane, young	un *giovane* ragazzo (a *young* boy)

* Adjectives ending in -*co* and -*go* may or may not retain the hard sound of the *c* or *g* in the plural: *bianco, bianca, bianchi, bianche* (white), but *greco, greca, greci, greche* (Greek).

antico, ancient	nell'*antico* palazzo (in the *ancient* palace)
primo, secondo, etc., first, second, etc.	la *prima* fermata (the *first* stop) la *seconda* colazione (lunch) [the *second* breakfast]

Observation on the adjectives just listed:

1. The meaning of an adjective may change according to its position. Compare:

il ragazzo *povero*	the *poor* boy (not rich)
il *povero* ragazzo	the *poor* boy (unfortunate)
l'amico *vecchio*	the *aged* friend
il *vecchio* amico	the *old* friend (of long standing)

In general, the adjective has its literal meaning when it follows the noun and a figurative meaning when it precedes it.

2. Adjectives which normally precede the noun may be placed after it for special emphasis:

Che viaggio *lungo*!   What a *long* journey!

Special Forms of *Bello, Buono, Grande*

When *bello, buono,* and *grande* are placed immediately before their noun, special forms are used.   In all other cases, these adjectives have their normal endings.   Compare:

È un *buon* ristorante? [Is a good restaurant?]	Is it a *good* restaurant?
Questo ristorante è *buono.*	This restaurant is *good.*
È *buono* questo ristorante? [Is good this restaurant?]	Is this restaurant *good*?

Bello

The special forms of *bello* are similar to the contractions formed by the prepositions *di* and *in* when used with the definite article.

	SING.	PL.	
MASC.	bel	bei	*bel* ragazzo, *bei* ragazzi *handsome* boy, *handsome* boys
	bello	begli	*bello* scaffale, *begli* scaffali *fine* bookcase, *fine* bookcases
	bell'	begl'	*bell'*insetto, *begl'*insetti *pretty* insect, *pretty* insects
FEM.	bella	belle	*bella* ragazza, *belle* ragazze *lovely* girl, *lovely* girls
	bell'	belle	*bell'*automobile, *belle* entrate *fine* car, *handsome* entrances

Observation:

Begl', masculine plural, is used only before a noun beginning with *i-*.

Buono

The special forms of *buono* in the singular are similar to the forms of the indefinite article.

	SING.	PL.	
MASC.	buon	buoni	*buon* posto, *buoni* posti *good* seat, *good* seats *buon* attore, *buoni* attori *good* actor, *good* actors
	buono	buoni	*buono* zio, *buoni* zii *good* uncle, *good* uncles
FEM.	buona	buone	*buona* madre, *buone* madri *good* mother, *good* mothers
	buon'		*buon'*analisi *good* analysis

Grande

    Grande becomes *gran* before a singular noun beginning with any consonant except *z* or *s* followed by a consonant: un *gran* libro (a good book), una *gran* donna (a wonderful woman), un *gran* pittore (a good painter). *Grand'* is the form used before a noun beginning with a vowel: un *grand'*uomo (a great man). The full form *grande* is also used in these cases for the sake of greater emphasis: un *grande* pittore (a great painter).

Adverbs

In English, adverbs are often formed by adding -*ly* to the adjective: clear, clear*ly*; recent, recent*ly*. In Italian, adverbs are formed in a similar way, by adding -*mente* to the feminine singular of the adjective. Study this table:

ADJECTIVE		ADVERB
MASC. SING.	FEM. SING.	
assoluto (absolute)	assoluta	assoluta*mente* (absolutely)
chiaro (clear)	chiara	chiara*mente* (clearly)
rapido (rapid)	rapida	rapida*mente* (rapidly)
recente (recent)	recente	recente*mente* (recently)

Lei parla troppo *rapidamente*.
You speak too quickly.

È *assolutamente* falso.
It is absolutely false.

Note that in adjectives ending in -*le* or -*re*, the final -*e* is dropped before adding -*mente*:

faci*le*, easy	facil*mente*, easily
regola*re*, regular	regolar*mente*, regularly

You should memorize the following list of common adverbs that do not end in -*mente*:

bene	well	Non mi sento *bene*. [Not to me I feel well.] I don't feel *well*.
male	badly, poorly	Si sente *male*. [To himself he feels badly.] He feels *sick*.

troppo	too much	Costa *troppo*. It costs *too much*.
molto	very, a lot	Mio padre è *molto* ricco. My father is *very* rich.
assai	very	Andiamo *assai* lontano. We are going *very* far.
tanto	so, so much, very much	Non *tanto*. Not *so much*. Egli canta *tanto* bene. He sings *so* well.
adagio	slowly	Parli *adagio*, per favore. Speak *slowly*, please.
presto	quickly, early	Venga *presto*. Come *quickly*. Ci alziamo sempre *presto*. [Ourselves we get up always early.] We always get up *early*.
sempre	always	Roma è *sempre* bella. Rome is *always* beautiful.
subito	immediately	Partiamo *subito*. We are leaving *immediately*.
spesso	often	Vado *spesso* a Roma. I go *often* to Rome.

Comparisons of Adjectives and Adverbs

Comparisons of Inequality

There are two ways of expressing comparison in English. You can add *-er* or *-est* to some adjectives and adverbs (sweet, sweet*er*, sweet*est*; soon, soon*er*, soon*est*). Or you can place the words "more" or "less," "most" or "least" before these and other adjectives and adverbs (beautiful, *more* or *less* beautiful, *most* or *least* beautiful; slowly, *more* or *less* slowly, *most* or *least* slowly).

In Italian there is only one way of expressing comparison. Place the words *più* (more), *il più* (most), or *meno* (less), *il meno* (least) before the adjective or adverb. In adjectives, the definite article in *il più* and *il meno* must agree with the noun.

Study the following table:

pesante, heavy	*più* pesante, heavier	*il più* pesante, heaviest
	meno pesante, less heavy	*il meno* pesante, least heavy
interessante, interesting	*più* interessante, more interesting	*il più* interessante, most interesting
	meno interessante, less interesting	*il meno* interessante, least interesting

La mia valigia è pesante, ma la sua è *più* pesante. La valigia di mio marito è *la più* pesante.
My suitcase is heavy, but yours is heavier. My husband's suitcase is the heaviest.

È stato un viaggio interessante. Il viaggio di Pietro è stato *meno* interessante. Il viaggio di Mario *il meno* interessante di tutti.
It was an interesting trip. Peter's trip was less interesting. Mario's trip the least interesting of all.

32

Per favore, parli *più* lentamente, *il più* lentamente possibile.
Please speak slowly, as slowly as possible.

Irregular Comparative Forms

While most adjectives and adverbs express comparison regularly, some very common adjectives and adverbs have irregular forms of comparison which are used more frequently than the regular ones.

ADJ.	buono, good	più buono or *migliore*, better	il più buono or *il migliore*, best
	cattivo, bad	più cattivo or *peggiore*, worse	il più cattivo or *il peggiore*, worst
	grande, big	più grande or *maggiore*, larger, greater	il più grande or *il maggiore*, largest, greatest
ADV.	bene, well	più bene or *meglio*, better	il più bene, or *il meglio*, best
	male, badly	più male, or *peggio*, worse	il più male or *il peggio*, worst

Questo è *il migliore* ristorante di* questa città.
This is the best restaurant in this city.

Lei guida *peggio* di me.
She drives worse than I.

The Absolute Superlative

Characteristic of Italian is the adjective or adverb which ends in -*issimo*. This form is called the absolute superlative because it implies no comparison. A similar absolute judgment is expressed in English when you say *very rich* or *extremely rich*, or when you use *excellent* instead of *the best*. Compare the meaning of

* Note that the word "in" when used after a superlative is translated by *di* in Italian.

"This book is excellent" with "This is the best book that I have read."

Add the suffix -*issimo* to the adjective or adverb after dropping the final vowel: pover*o* (poor), pover*issimo* (extremely poor); mal*e* (badly), mal*issimo* (very badly); ricc*o* (rich), ricch*issimo* (very rich).* For adverbs which end in -*mente*, the -*issimo* is added to the adjective before -*mente*: lento (slow), lent*issimo* (very slow), lent*issima*mente (very slowly). Remember that the form of the adjective to which -*mente* is added is the feminine singular: lentissim*a*.

È un'opera *interessantissima.*
It is a *very interesting* opera.

Carissimo amico!
My *very dear* friend!

Queste fragole sono *dolcissime.*
These strawberries are *very sweet.*

Lei parla *benissimo.*
You speak *extremely well.*

The Word "Than"

The word *than* used in comparisons (He is richer *than* you are) is translated by either *di* or *che* in Italian. An easy rule to remember is that *di* is used before *nouns, pronouns,* and *numerals,* while *che* is used everywhere else. Observe the following examples:

Roma è più bella *di* Firenze. (noun)
Rome is more beautiful *than* Florence.

Mio padre è più ricco *di* me. (pronoun)
My father is richer *than* I.

Non voglio spendere più *di* mille lire. (numeral)
I don't want to spend more *than* 1,000 lire.

---

* For adjectives ending in -*co* or -*go* insert an *h* before adding -*issimo* to keep the hard sound of *c* or *g*: ricco (rich), ricc*h*issimo (very rich), lungo (long), lung*h*issimo (very long).

But: Questa strada è più lunga *che* larga.   (adjective)
This street is longer *than* (it is) wide.

È meglio partire subito *che* aspettare.   (verb)
It is better to leave at once *than* to wait.

Parlo più spesso con lui *che* con suo fratello.   (preposition)
I speak more often with him *than* with his brother.

Comparisons of Equality

The "as . . . as" of comparisons of equality (I am *as* tall *as* my brother) is translated in Italian either by *così . . . come* or by *tanto . . . quanto*.   As in English, the two words are placed around the adjective or adverb: *così* lungo *come* (*as* long *as*), *tanto* presto *quanto* (*as* early *as*).   But contrary to English, the first term of the comparison, the *così* or the *tanto*, may be omitted without any change in meaning.

La nostra stanza è *così* cara *come* la loro.
La nostra stanza è cara *come* la loro.
Our room is *as* expensive *as* theirs.

Sono *tanto* ricco *quanto* lui.
Sono ricco *quanto* lui.
I am *as* rich *as* he.

Expressing Possession

In English, you can say either "the teacher's book" or "the book of the teacher." There is no form corresponding to the apostrophe s in Italian. A form comparable to "the book of the teacher" is used.

le case *di* mio padre   il palazzo *del* re
[the houses *of* my father]   [the palace *of the* king]
my father's houses   the king's palace

Possessive Adjectives

In Italian, the possessive adjective is almost always preceded by the definite article. Study the two words together as a unit.

MASC. SING.	FEM. SING.	MASC. PL.	FEM. PL.	
il mio	la mia	i miei	le mie	my
il tuo	la tua	i tuoi	le tue	your (fam. sing.)
il suo	la sua	i suoi	le sue	his, her, its, your (polite sing.)
il nostro	la nostra	i nostri	le nostre	our
il vostro	la vostra	i vostri	le vostre	your (fam. sing. & pl.)
il loro	la loro	i loro	le loro	their, your (polite pl.)

Observations on possessive adjectives:

1. The endings *-o, -a, -i, -e* are the same as those of other adjectives which end in *-o* in the masculine singular.

2. The masculine plural forms *i miei, i tuoi, i suoi* are irregular.

3. *Loro* is invariable.

4. Possessive adjectives agree in gender and number with the noun they accompany, that is, with the thing possessed:

Dove sono *le nostre* valigie?
Where are *our* suitcases?

Signore, ecco *il suo* passaporto.
Sir, here is *your* passport.

36

Signora, ecco *il suo* passaporto.
Madam, here is *your* passport.

Ecco *i miei* fratelli e *le mie* sorelle.
Here are *my* brothers and *my* sisters.

Ecco *il suo* soprabito e *i suoi* guanti.
Here is *your* overcoat and *your* gloves.

5. The definite article is omitted:

(a) before unmodified words of family relationship in the singular:

Mio padre è vecchio.   *Sua* figlia è cortese.
My father is old.   *His* daughter is polite.

(b) after the word *questo* and after numerals:

Questo mio orologio si è fermato.
[This my watch has stopped.]
This watch of mine has stopped.

Due miei amici non sono ancora arrivati.
[Two my friends not have yet arrived.]
Two friends of mine have not yet arrived.

(c) when the possessive stands alone:

Di chi è questo libro?   È *mio.*
[Of whom is this book?   Is mine.]
Whose book is this?   It's *mine.*

Quel cane è *nostro.*
That dog is *ours.*

6. Sometimes, contrary to English usage, the possessive adjective itself is omitted. This happens especially with parts of the body or with articles of clothing about whose ownership there can be no doubt.

Ho perduto *i* guanti.
[I have lost *the* gloves.]
I have lost *my* gloves.

Ha perduto *la* testa.
He lost *his* head.

Demonstrative Adjectives and Pronouns

Demonstrative Adjectives

The demonstrative adjectives *questo* (this) and *quello* (that) refer, as in English, to both persons and things. They always agree with the noun they accompany.

Questo has the four adjective endings *-o, -a, -i, -e*, with which you are already familiar. *Questo* and *questa* become *quest'* before a noun beginning with a vowel. *Questi* and *queste* may become *quest'* before plural nouns beginning with *i* and *e* respectively.

	SING.	PL.	
MASC.	questo	questi	*questo* fiore, *questi* fiori this flower, these flowers
	quest'		*quest'*albergo, *questi* alberghi this hotel, these hotels
FEM.	questa	queste	*questa* bambola, *queste* bambole this doll, these dolls
	quest'		*quest'*azione, *queste* azioni this action, these actions

*Quest'*individui amano cantare.   These individuals like to sing.
Mi piace *quest'*aperitivo.   I like this apéritif.
[To me is pleasing this apéritif.]

Questa ragazza balla bene.   This girl dances well.
Questo treno è lento.   This train is slow.

Quello, when it precedes its noun or adjective, has the same forms as *bello* when *bello* precedes the noun.

38

	SING.	PL.	
MASC.	quel	quei	*Quel* ragazzo non è italiano. *That* boy is not Italian. *Quei* pacchi sono pesanti. *Those* packages are heavy.
	quell'	quegli	Non abita più a *quell'*indirizzo. He no longer lives at *that* address. Non conosco *quegli* uomini. I don't know *those* men.
	quello	quegli	*Quello* spettacolo comincia alle 4. *That* show begins at 4. *Quegli* studenti sono stranieri. *Those* students are foreigners.
FEM.	quella	quelle	*Quella* signora è americana. *That* lady is American. *Quelle* montagne sono alte. *Those* mountains are high.
	quell'	quelle	*Quell'*automobile è bella. *That* car is beautiful. *Quelle* albicocche sono deliziose. *Those* apricots are delicious.

Observation:

Quegli (masc. pl.) becomes *quegl'* before a masculine plural noun beginning with *i*: *quegl'*italiani (those Italians).

Questo and *Quello* as Pronouns

When used as pronouns, *questo* means "this" or "this one," *quello* "that" or "that one." They can refer to both persons and things. *Questi* (this one, this man) and *quegli* (that one, that man) are masculine singular pronouns which refer only to persons.

Questo mi piace più di *quello.*
[*This* to me is pleasing more than *that.*]
I like *this one* better than *that one.*

Quello che ha detto è vero.
[*That* which (he) has said is true.]
What he said is true.

Quali guanti preferisce sua moglie?   *Quelli.*
Which gloves does your wife prefer?   *Those.*

Questi non dice la verità.
This man does not tell the truth.

Questi è mio padre, *quegli* mio marito.
This one is my father, *that one* my husband.

The Pronoun *Ciò*

Ciò (this, that) is very often used instead of *questo* and *quello* to refer to things.

Ciò è falso.
This is false.

Ciò che ha detto è vero.
[That which (he) has said is true.]
What he said is true.

Personal Pronouns

In Italian, as in English, pronouns have different forms according to their use and position in a sentence.

Subject Pronouns

	SING.		PL.	
1ST PERS.	io	I	noi	we
2ND PERS.	tu	you (fam.)	voi	you (fam.)
3RD PERS.	egli	he	loro	they
	lui	he		
	lei	she		
	esso	it (masc.)	essi	they (masc.)
	essa	it (fem.)	esse	they (fem.)
	Lei	you (polite)	Loro	you (polite)

Observations on subject pronouns:

1. The pronoun *ella* (she) is no longer in current use. *Esso* and *essa* with the meaning of "he" and "she" are also going out of use, and are replaced more and more frequently by *lui* and *lei*.

2. The Italian pronouns which translate the English "you" are *tu, voi, Lei,* and *Loro*. Since *tu* is used in addressing members of the family and close friends, and *voi* in the singular has a somewhat condescending connotation, the tourist will probably use only *Lei* (sing.) and *Loro* (pl.). Concentrate on these forms.

3. Since Italian verbs have endings that indicate the person, it is not necessary to use the subject pronoun with verbs as in English.

Viaggiamo spesso.   Fuma ?
We travel often.   Do you smoke ?

4. The subject pronoun *io* is used when contrast or emphasis is involved.

41

Parto domani mattina.
I am leaving tomorrow morning.

Io parto domani, ma mio fratello parte la settimana prossima.
I'm leaving tomorrow, but my brother is leaving next week.

Direct and Indirect Object Pronouns

In English, the object pronouns (me, you, him, her, it, us, them) are either direct (He takes *it*) or indirect (He gives *me* the book, i.e., He gives the book *to me*). The same is true in Italian, except that in several cases object pronouns have a different form when they are direct and when they are indirect. Compare the two tables:

		DIRECT OBJECT PRONOUNS		INDIRECT OBJECT PRONOUNS
SING.	1st person	mi	me	mi (to) me
	2nd person	ti	you (familiar)	ti (to) you (familiar)
	3rd person	lo	him, it (masc.)	gli (to) him, it (masc.)
		la	her, it (fem.)	le (to) her, it (fem.)
		La	you (polite)	Le (to) you (polite)
PL.	1st person	ci	us	ci (to) us
	2nd person	vi	you (familiar)	vi (to) you (familiar)
	3rd person	li	them (masc.)	loro (to) them (masc.)
		le	them (fem.)	loro (to) them (fem.)
		Li	you (polite) (masc.)	Loro (to) you (polite) (masc.)
		Le	you (polite) (fem.)	Loro (to) you (polite) (fem.)

Ci hanno dato questo libro.   (indir. obj.)
They gave *us* this book.

Mi dica la verità.   (indir. obj.)
Tell *me* the truth.

Lo conosco molto bene.   (dir. obj.)
I know *him* very well.

Ora non *la* vedo, ma *le* ho parlato dieci minuti fa.   (dir. obj.)
Now I don't see *her*, but I spoke *to her* ten minutes ago.   (indir. obj.)

Observations:

1. Since you will probably use only *Lei* and *Loro* to translate the English "you," concentrate on the direct and indirect object pronouns which correspond to them: *La* (you) and *Le* (to you), *Li*, *Le* (you) and *Loro* (to you). These forms are often capitalized in writing to distinguish them from *la* (her), *le* (to her), *li*, *le* (them), and *loro* (to them).

Non *Le* possiamo dare questa lettera.
We can't give *you* this letter.

2. Object pronouns, with the exception of *loro*, precede the verb.

Li abbiamo visti e abbiamo parlato *loro*.
We saw *them* and we spoke *to them*.

3. But if the verb is an infinitive or a participle, the pronoun follows it and is written as one word with it. The final -*e* of the infinitive is dropped before adding a pronoun. *Loro* always stands alone.

Voglio sentir*lo*.
I want to hear *it*.

Vedendo*lo*, *lo* riconobbi.
Seeing *him*, I recognized *him*.

Voglio dare *loro* il libro.
I want to give *them* the book.

4. The object pronoun also follows the verb and is written as one word with it in an affirmative command, but *not* with commands given to persons addressed as *Lei* and *Loro*.

Dite*mi* la verità.   (voi)
Tell *me* the truth.

Mi dica la verità.   (Lei)
Tell *me* the truth.

5. *Lo* and *la* become *l'* before a verb beginning with a vowel or with *h*.

*L'*accettiamo volentieri.
We accept *it* gladly.

*L'*ho visto ieri.
I saw *him* yesterday.

Direct and Indirect Object Pronouns with the Same Verb

When a verb has both a direct and an indirect object pronoun, the indirect precedes the direct.   Note that the *i* of *mi, ti, ci,* and *vi* changes to *e* before *lo, la, li,* and *le.*   *Gli* and *le* both become *glie* before *lo, la, li,* and *le.*   The *glie* and the pronoun following it are written as one word.

Me lo dice.
He tells *it to me.*

Glieli vendo con piacere.
I sell *them to you* (or to him, or to her) with pleasure.

Stressed Forms of the Personal Pronouns

These are the pronouns used after prepositions:

SING.		PL.	
per *me*	for *me*	fra di *noi*	among *us*
con *te*	with *you* (fam. sing.)	prima di *voi*	before *you* (fam. pl.)
di *lui*	of *him*	vicino a *loro*	near *them* (masc. & fem.)
con *lei*	with *her*		
a *Lei*	to *you* (polite sing.)	a *Loro*	to *you* (polite pl.)

How to Avoid the Use of Double Pronouns

You can avoid object pronouns (I gave *it* to *him*) by replacing them with nouns (I gave *the book* to *John*). You can avoid using two pronouns with the same verb by replacing one of them with a noun (I gave *it* to *John*).

Me lo diede. (2 obj. pro.)	*Mi* diede il libro. (1 obj. pro.)
He gave *it to me.*	He gave *me* the book.
Gliela mostrai. (2 obj. pro.)	*Gli* mostrai la casa. (1 obj. pro.)
I showed *it to him.*	I showed *him* the house.

Instead of the indirect object pronoun you can use the stressed form of the pronoun with the preposition *a* (to). In this way you avoid combinations such as *glielo*, *me lo*, etc.

Me lo diede.	*Lo* diede *a me.*
He gave *it to me.*	He gave *it to me.*
Gliela mostrai.	*La* mostrai *a lui.*
I showed *it to him.*	I showed *it to him.*

Table of Personal Pronouns

You will find the following tables useful in reviewing the personal pronouns. For the sake of completeness we are including the *reflexive pronouns* here too. You will need to know them when you study reflexive verbs on page 81.

The second table, on page 48, illustrates the changes in personal pronouns which occur when there is both a direct and an indirect object pronoun used with the same verb.

TABLE OF PRONOUNS

| | UNSTRESSED | | | | STRESSED | |
	SUBJECT	OBJECT DIRECT	OBJECT INDIRECT	REFLEXIVE		
SING.						
1st person	io — I	mi — me	mi — to me	mi — myself, to myself	me	me
2nd person	tu — you (fam.)	ti — you	ti — to you	ti — yourself, to yourself	te	you
3rd person	egli, lui — he	lo — him, it	gli — to him, it	si — himself, herself, itself, to himself, etc.	lui	him
	lei — she	la — her, it	le — to her, it		lei	her
	esso — it (masc.)				esso	it
	essa — it (fem.)				essa	it
					se	himself, herself, itself
	Lei — you (polite)	La — you	Le — to you	si — yourself, to yourself	Lei	you
					se	yourself

| | | UNSTRESSED | | | STRESSED |
| | | OBJECT | | | |
	SUBJECT	DIRECT	INDIRECT	REFLEXIVE	
PL.					
1st person	noi we	ci us	ci to us	ci ourselves, to ourselves	noi us
2nd person	voi you (fam.)	vi you	vi to you	vi yourself, yourselves, to yourself, etc.	voi you
3rd person	loro they	li them	loro to them	si themselves, to themselves	loro them
	essi they (masc.)	le them			essi them
	esse they (fem.)				esse them
					se themselves
	Loro you (polite)	Li you	Loro to you	si yourselves, to yourselves	Loro you
		Le you			se yourselves

Relative Position of Pronouns

When a direct and an indirect pronoun are used together, the indirect precedes the direct and undergoes the following changes:

me lo	me la	me li	me le	him, her, it, them to me
te lo	te la	te li	te le	him, her, it, them to you (fam. sing.)
glielo	gliela	glieli	gliele	him, her, it, them to him, her, it, you (pol. sing.)
se lo	se la	se li	se le	him, her, it, them to himself, herself, itself, yourself (pol.)
ce lo	ce la	ce li	ce le	him, her, it, them to us
ve lo	ve la	ve li	ve le	him, her, it, them to you (fam. pl.)
se lo	se la	se li	se le	him, her, it, them to themselves, yourselves (pol.)

The indirect pronoun *loro* (*Loro*) is always placed after the verb:

Egli lo (la, li, le) dà *loro*.

He gives him (her, them, etc.) *to them*.

Egli lo dà *Loro*.

He gives it *to you* (pol. pl.).

Negatives

In Italian, any sentence can be made negative by placing *non* (not) before the verb.

Questa città *non* è molto grande.
This city is *not* very large.

Non parlo molto bene.
[Not I speak very well.]
I do *not* speak very well.

If there is an object pronoun preceding the verb, *non* is placed before the pronoun and not directly before the verb.

Non lo vedo.
[*Not* him I see.]
I don't see him.

Non mi può chiamare un tassì?
[*Not* to me can call a taxi?]
Can't you call me a taxi?

Other important negatives are:

non . . . mai   never
non . . . più   no longer
non . . . niente   nothing
non . . . nessuno   nobody
non . . . neanche   not even
non . . . nè . . . nè   neither . . . nor

Non sono *mai* stato in Italia.
[*Not* am *ever* been in Italy.]
I have *never* been in Italy.

Non vedo *niente*.
[*Not* I see *nothing*.]
I see *nothing*.

Non è venuto *nessuno.*
[*Not* is come *nobody.*]
Nobody came.

Non abita *più* qui.
[*Not* he lives *more* here.]
He *no longer* lives here.

Non è venuto *neanche* il presidente.
[*Not* is come *not even* the president.]
Not even the president came.

Non abbiamo visitato *nè* Roma *nè* Firenze.
[*Not* we have visited *neither* Rome *nor* Florence.]
We visited *neither* Rome *nor* Florence.

Observations:

Negative words, such as *niente* (nothing), *mai* (never), etc., are almost always used with *non*. *Non* is placed before the verb, the other negative word after the verb.

Negative words may also stand alone, as in the sentence:

Chi è venuto con Lei? *Nessuno.*
Who came with you? *No one.*

Che, Cui, Chi

Che as Conjunction

In English, the conjunction *that* is frequently omitted. (*I think that he will come* is often abbreviated to *I think he will come.*) In Italian, the conjunction *che* must be expressed.

Credo *che* verrà.
I think (*that*) he will come.

Sa *che* non sono ancora arrivati?
Do you know (*that*) they haven't arrived yet?

Che as Relative Pronoun

In addition to being a conjunction, *che* is also a relative pronoun (*who, which, that, whom*). It refers to either persons or things, and can be used as either subject or object. It is the most important of the relative pronouns.

È lo stesso cameriere *che* era qui ieri. (refers to a person, subject)
He is the same waiter *who* was here yesterday.

Ecco un vestito *che* non costa molto. (refers to a thing, subject)
Here is a dress *which* doesn't cost much.

L'uomo *che* cerca non abita più qui. (refers to a person, object)
The man *whom* you are looking for no longer lives here.

Non trovo il dizionario *che* ho comprato ieri. (refers to a thing, object)
I don't find the dictionary *which* I bought yesterday.

The Relative Pronoun *Cui*

After prepositions, a special form of the relative pronoun is used: *cui*. *Cui*, too, stands for either persons or things.

L'uomo *con cui* parlo è il direttore. (refers to a person)
The man *with whom* I am speaking is the director.

La porta *da cui* si esce è a sinistra.   (refers to a thing)
The door *by which* one leaves is to the left.

The Interrogative Pronoun *Chi*

Che is often confused with *chi*.   Use *chi* as an interrogative to refer to persons.

Chi è quell'uomo?
Who is that man?

Con *chi* sei venuto?
With *whom* did you come?

Conjunctions

Although we are emphasizing simple straight-forward expressions, there will be need from time to time to use longer, more complicated sentences. For this purpose you should become acquainted with the following list of basic conjunctions.

e	and	Ho veduto questo quadro *e* l'ho comprato.
		I saw this picture *and* I bought it.
o	or	Vuole andare al cinema *o* preferisce il teatro?
		Do you want to go to the movies *or* do you prefer the theater?
ma	but	Vorrei comprarlo *ma* non ho denari con me.
		I would like to buy it *but* I don't have money with me.
quando	when	Partirò *quando* parte Lei.
		I shall leave *when* you are leaving.
mentre	while	Io andrò a Roma *mentre* mio marito resta qui.
		I shall go to Rome *while* my husband stays here.
se	if	Lo comprerò *se* mi piace.
		I shall buy it *if* I like it.
perchè	because	Prendo l'ombrello *perchè* piove.
		I'm taking the umbrella *because* it's raining.
benchè	although (followed by subjunctive)	Uscirò *benchè* sia tardi.
		I shall go out *although* it is late.

Verbs

Before proceeding to study this section, you should become acquainted with the material covered in pages 97 to 101 of the Glossary of Grammatical Terms. Although you may not remember everything at a first reading, this material will help you to understand special constructions and expressions as you come to them.

Comparison of English and Italian Verbs

Italian verbs are more complicated than English ones. In English, there are very few changes in ending, and those that do occur are relatively uniform: I sing, he sing*s*; I take, he take*s*. In Italian, each person has its own distinctive ending: io parl*o* (*I* speak), tu parl*i* (*you* speak). Since the subject pronoun is very often omitted in Italian, failure to employ the correct ending results in misunderstanding: parl*o* (*I* speak), parl*a* (*he* speaks).

Another aspect in which Italian verbs are more complicated than English is the greater number of tenses used in Italian. You will notice this when we speak of the various past tenses and of the subjunctive mood. Though it is possible to avoid some difficulties by using short, simple sentences, it is necessary to be acquainted with the various aspects of the Italian verb for understanding the spoken and the written language. In the pages which follow, we shall always distinguish between those forms which must be memorized from the start and those which you can study at a later date.

The Three Conjugations

All Italian verbs belong to one of three conjugations. Since the various endings which a particular verb takes are determined

54

by the conjugation to which it belongs, you must pay special attention to this point. By classifying verbs into conjugations it is easier to remember their many forms.

The conjugation to which an Italian verb belongs is determined by the ending of its infinitive (that is, of the form which corresponds to the English "to walk," "to have," etc.).

Verbs ending in -*are* belong to the *first conjugation*

,,   ,,   ,,   -*ere*   ,,   ,,   ,,   *second conjugation*

,,   ,,   ,,   -*ire*   ,,   ,,   ,,   *third conjugation*

All verbs which belong to the same conjugation (except irregular ones) are conjugated like the model verb of that conjugation. Our model verbs are:

parlare (to speak)	*first conjugation*
vendere (to sell)	*second conjugation*
partire (to depart)	*third conjugation*
capire (to understand)	*third conjugation*

Regular verbs ending in -*are* will therefore take the same endings as the model verb *parlare*. Regular verbs in -*ere* and -*ire* will take the same endings as the models *vendere* and *partire* or *capire* respectively.

Irregular verbs will be treated separately, tense by tense.

The Present Tense

Comparison of Present Tense in English and Italian

In English, we have three different ways of expressing an action in the present. We can say "I walk," "I am walking," or "I do walk." The three forms are distinguished by slight differences in meaning. In Italian, on the other hand, the present tense conveys all three meanings of the English.

First Conjugation

Memorize the present tense of the model verb *parlare* (to speak):

(io)	parl*o*	I speak, am speaking, do speak
(tu)	parl*i*	you (fam. sing.) speak, are speaking, do speak

(egli) parl*a*   he (she, it) speaks, is speaking, does speak; you
                  (polite sing.) speak, are speaking, do speak
(noi) parl*iamo* we speak, are speaking, do speak
(voi) parl*ate* you (fam. pl., also sing.) speak, are speaking,
                  do speak
(loro) parl*ano* they speak, are speaking, do speak; you (polite
                  pl.) speak, are speaking, do speak

Second Conjugation

Memorize the present tense of the model verb *vendere* (to sell):

(io)   vend*o*   I sell, am selling, do sell
(tu)   vend*i*   you (fam. sing.) sell, are selling, do sell
(egli) vend*e*   he (she, it) sells, is selling, does sell; you (polite
                   sing.) sell, are selling, do sell
(noi) vend*iamo* we sell, are selling, do sell
(voi) vend*ete*   you (fam. pl., also sing.) sell, are selling, do
                   sell
(loro) vend*ono*   they sell, are selling, do sell; you (polite pl.)
                   sell, are selling, do sell

Third Conjugation

Memorize the present tense of the model verb *partire* (to
depart):

(io)   part*o*   I depart, am departing, do depart
(tu)   part*i*   you (fam. sing.) depart, are departing, do
                   depart
(egli) part*e*   he (she, it) departs, is departing, does depart;
                   you (polite sing.) depart, are departing, do
                   depart
(noi) part*iamo* we depart, are departing, do depart
(voi) part*ite*   you (fam. pl., also sing.) depart, are departing,
                   do depart
(loro) part*ono*   they depart, are departing, do depart; you
                   (polite, pl.) depart, are departing, do depart

The third conjugation differs from the other two conjugations because not all its regular verbs follow the pattern of the model verb. The majority of third conjugation verbs insert the suffix -*isc*- before the ending in all persons of the singular and in the third person plural. There is no easy rule by which you can recognize which third conjugation verbs are like *partire* and which are like *capire* (to understand). When you learn new verbs try to remember to which category they belong.

Memorize the present tense of *capire* (to understand) as a model for third conjugation verbs of the second category:

(io) cap*isco*	I understand, am understanding, do understand
(tu) cap*isci*	you (fam. sing.) understand, do understand, are understanding
(egli) cap*isce*	he (she, it) understands, is understanding, does understand; you (polite sing.) understand, are understanding, do understand
(noi) cap*iamo*	we understand, are understanding, do understand
(voi) cap*ite*	you (fam. pl., also sing.) understand, are understanding, do understand
(loro) cap*iscono*	they understand, are understanding, do understand; you (polite pl.) understand, are understanding, do understand

Observations on the present tense:

1. If you prefer, you may omit the second person singular form in memorizing, since you will not be likely to use it.

2. To help you remember the endings of the present tense for the three conjugations note that:

(a) in all three conjugations, the first person singular ends in -*o*; the second person singular in -*i*; the first person plural in -*iamo*.

(b) the second person plural ending has the characteristic

vowel of the infinitive: parl*a*te, vend*e*te, cap*i*te, but is otherwise the same in all three conjugations.

(c)   in the second and third conjugations, all endings are alike, except for the second person plural: vend*e*te, cap*i*te.   The suffix -*isc*-, which appears in third conjugation verbs, does not technically count as an ending.

(d)   in the first conjugation, you find the same vowel *a* in the third person, both singular and plural: parl*a*, parl*a*no.

The Present Tense of Commonly Used Irregular Verbs

Some of the verbs most commonly used in Italian are not con-jugated like the model verbs.   They are irregular and must be memorized.

Infinitive	*io*	*tu*	*egli*	*noi*	*voi*	*loro*
avere (to have)	ho	hai	ha	abbiamo	avete	hanno
essere (to be)	sono	sei	è	siamo	siete	sono
andare (to go)	vado	vai	va	andiamo	andate	vanno
dare (to give)	do	dai	dà	diamo	date	danno
*fare (to do)	faccio	fai	fa	facciamo	fate	fanno
stare (to be)	sto	stai	sta	stiamo	state	stanno
dovere (to have to)	devo	devi	deve	dobbiamo	dovete	devono
potere (to be able)	posso	puoi	può	possiamo	potete	possono
sapere (to know)	so	sai	sa	sappiamo	sapete	sanno
*bere (to drink)	bevo	bevi	beve	beviamo	bevete	bevono
tenere (to hold)	tengo	tieni	tiene	teniamo	tenete	tengono
*dire (to say, tell)	dico	dici	dice	diciamo	dite	dicono
venire (to come)	vengo	vieni	viene	veniamo	venite	vengono
*uscire (to go out)	esco	esci	esce	usciamo	uscite	escono

* Some irregularities can be explained by keeping in mind that a number of verbs originally had another infinitive form: dire, dicere; fare, facere; uscire, escire; bere, bevere.

The Progressive Present

In studying the present tense in Italian, you no doubt noticed that *parlo* was translated both as "I speak" and as "I am speaking." The form "I am speaking" is more vivid than "I speak" because the action is represented as going on, as being in progress. However, there is no time difference between the two forms, so that we can say either "The boat leaves" or "The boat is leaving" and refer to exactly the same time. Both in English and in Italian, the present participle (the verb form ending in *-ing*: "taking," "looking") is used in forming the progressive.

The Present Participle

In Italian, the present participle is formed by dropping the infinitive ending *-are, -ere, -ire,* and adding *-ando* to verbs of the first conjugation, *-endo* to verbs of the second and the third.

compr*are* (to buy)	compr*ando* (buying)
vend*ere* (to sell)	vend*endo* (selling)
fin*ire* (to finish)	fin*endo* (finishing)

The Use of *Stare*

Of the two Italian verbs which mean "to be," the one which is used in forming the progressive is *stare.**

Sto finendo questa lettera.	*I am finishing* this letter.
Il piroscafo *sta partendo.*	The boat *is leaving.*
Stiamo facendo colazione.	*We are having* breakfast.
Che cosa *sta scrivendo?*	What *are you writing?*
A chi *sta scrivendo?*	To whom *are you writing?*

The Imperative or Command Form

To distinguish between the different verb forms used for giving commands, we must go back to the different pronouns which all mean "you" in Italian: *tu, Lei, voi, Loro.* Since you will be using

* Other differences in the use of *essere* and *stare* will be discussed on page 89.

the polite form (*Lei* and *Loro*) most frequently, we shall study that first.   Concentrate on the singular.

Third Person Command Forms

parlare (to speak)	parl*i* (polite sing.)—speak! parl*ino* (polite pl.)—speak!
vedere (to see)	ved*a* (polite sing.)—see! ved*ano* (polite pl.)—see!
partire (to depart)	part*a* (polite sing.)—leave! part*ano* (polite pl.)—leave!
finire (to finish)	finisc*a* (polite sing.)—finish! finisc*ano* (polite pl.)—finish!

Observe that those third conjugation verbs which insert -*isc*- in the present, do so in the command form as well.

Many of the more common verbs have irregular command forms for the polite singular and plural.   Here are the most useful:

fare (to do)	faccia (polite sing.)—do! facciano (polite pl.)—do!
andare (to go)	vada (polite sing.)—go! vadano (polite pl.)—go!
dare (to give)	dia (polite sing.)—give! diano (polite pl.)—give!
stare (to be)	stia (polite sing.)—be! stiano (polite pl.)—be!
bere (to drink)	beva (polite sing.)—drink! bevano (polite pl.)—drink!
dire (to say)	dica (polite sing.)—say! dicano (polite pl.)—say!
tenere (to hold, to take)	tenga (polite sing.)—take! tengano (polite pl.)—take!

To soften a command add the expressions *per favore* or *per piacere* ("please").

Apra la finestra, *per piacere.*	Open the window, please.
Mi porti un altro bicchiere, *per favore.*	Bring me another glass, please.

To avoid the command form altogether use the expressions *Mi faccia il piacere di* ("Do me the favor of") or *Vorrebbe* ("Would you") with the infinitive.

Mi faccia il piacere di aprire la finestra.	Please open the window.
Vorrebbe aprire la finestra, *per piacere?*	Would you please open the window?
Mi faccia il piacere di parlare più lentamente.	Please speak more slowly.
Vorrebbe parlare più lentamente, *per piacere?*	Would you please speak more slowly?

First Person Plural Commands

The first person plural command ("Let's go!" "Let's sing!") is always the same as the present in Italian.

Andiamo! (Let's go!)	*Leggiamo!* (Let's read!)
Cantiamo! (Let's sing!)	*Corriamo!* (Let's run!)

Familiar Command Forms

The command forms for *tu* and *voi* are identical with the present tense forms, except that in verbs of the first conjugation the -*i* ending of the *tu* form changes to -*a*.

parlare (to speak)	parl*a*! (fam. sing.)—speak! parlate! (fam. pl., also sing.)—speak!
vedere (to see)	vedi! (fam. sing.)—see! vedete! (fam. pl., also sing.)—see!

| *partire* (to depart) | parti! (fam. sing.)—depart!
partite! (fam. pl., also sing.)—
depart! |
| *finire* (to finish) | finisci! (fam. sing.)—finish!
finite! (fam. pl., also sing.)—
finish! |

For irregular verbs only the following forms must be learned, since they are different from the present tense:

fare (to do)	fa' (fam. sing.)—do!
dare (to give)	da' (fam. sing.)—give!
stare (to be)	sta' (fam. sing.)—be!
andare (to go)	va' (fam. sing.)—go!
dire (to say)	di' (fam. sing.)—say!

Review Table of Command Forms

	FIRST CONJUGATION	SECOND CONJUGATION	THIRD CONJUGATION
(fam. sing.)	parla	vendi	parti
(polite sing.)	parli	venda	parta
(first person pl.)	parliamo	vendiamo	partiamo
(fam. pl., also sing.)	parlate	vendete	partite
(polite pl.)	parlino	vendano	partano

The Present Perfect Tense

In Italian, as in English, there are several ways of expressing what happened in the past. The most useful of the past tenses in Italian is the present perfect, which, as far as meaning is concerned, corresponds most closely to the simple English past: "I went," "I left," "I bought," although it is, in form, more closely related to the English present perfect: "I have gone," "I have left," "I have bought." The present perfect tense consists of two parts: the present tense of the helping verb (*avere* (to have) or *essere* (to be)) and the past participle.

The Past Participle

In Italian, the past participle is formed by dropping the infinitive ending -*are*, -*ere*, -*ire* and adding -*ato* to verbs of the first conjugation, -*uto* to verbs of the second conjugation, and -*ito* to verbs of the third conjugation.

and*are* (to go)	and*ato* (gone)
ved*ere* (to see)	ved*uto* (seen)
sent*ire* (to hear)	sent*ito* (heard)

Many past participles, especially in the second conjugation, are irregular. Here are some of the most common:

nascere (to be born)	nato (born)
scrivere (to write)	scritto (written)
leggere (to read)	letto (read)
fàre (to do, to make)	fatto (done, made)
dire (to say)	detto (said)
morire (to die)	morto (dead)
rispondere (to answer)	risposto (answered)
venire (to come)	venuto (come)
conoscere (to know)	conosciuto (known)
scendere (to go down)	sceso (gone down)
chiudere (to close)	chiuso (closed)
rompere (to break)	rotto (broken)

The Helping Verbs *Avere* and *Essere*

The Italian present perfect, an otherwise "easy" tense, presents one difficulty: the speaker must know whether the helping verb to be used in a particular case is *essere* (to be) or *avere* (to have). The general rule is that verbs of motion which do not take a direct object ("I *went* to the dentist") are conjugated with *essere*, while other verbs are conjugated with *avere*.

Since it may be difficult for you to determine which are the verbs of motion that do not take a direct object, simply remember a few of the most common verbs used with *essere*. Here is a list:

entrare (to enter)	uscire (to go out)
partire (to depart)	andare (to go)
nascere (to be born)	morire (to die)
venire (to come)	scendere (to go down)

The past participle of a verb conjugated with *essere* actually becomes a kind of adjective. It is therefore natural that it must agree with the subject.

Maria è andat*a*.	Mary has gone.
Giovanni è andat*o*.	John has gone.

The Present Perfect of the Model Verbs

FIRST CONJUGATION

ho parlato	I spoke, I have spoken
hai parlato	you (fam. sing.) spoke, have spoken
ha parlato	he (she, it) spoke, has spoken; you (polite sing.) spoke, have spoken
abbiamo parlato	we spoke, have spoken
avete parlato	you (fam. pl., also sing.) spoke, have spoken
hanno parlato	they spoke, have spoken; you (polite pl.) spoke, have spoken

SECOND CONJUGATION

ho scritto*	I wrote, have written
hai scritto	you (fam. sing.) wrote, have written
ha scritto	he (she, it) wrote, has written; you (polite sing.) wrote, have written
abbiamo scritto	we wrote, have written
avete scritto	you (fam. pl., also sing.) wrote, have written
hanno scritto	they wrote, have written; you (polite pl.) wrote, have written

* *Scrivere* has an irregular past participle. We are using *scrivere* as a model verb for the sake of variety.

THIRD CONJUGATION

sono* partito (-a)	I departed, have departed
sei partito (-a)	you (fam. sing.) departed, have departed
è partito (-a)	he (she, it) departed, has departed; you (polite sing.) departed, have departed
siamo partiti (-e)	we departed, have departed
siete partiti (-e)	you (fam. pl., also sing.) departed, have
siete partito (-a)	departed
sono partiti (-e)	they departed, have departed; you (polite pl.) departed, have departed

The Past Definite Tense

Though the present perfect tense is probably the most useful of the past tenses for the beginner, it is also important for you to be acquainted with the past definite or preterit. This tense is often used interchangeably with the present perfect, especially in some parts of Italy. It is more difficult than the present perfect because you have to learn a set of new endings and also because a large number of verbs are irregular in this tense.

The Past Definite of the Model Verbs

FIRST CONJUGATION

parlai	I spoke
parlasti	you (fam. sing.) spoke
parlò	he (she, it) spoke; you (polite sing.) spoke
parlammo	we spoke
parlaste	you (fam. pl., also sing.) spoke
parlarono	they spoke; you (polite pl.) spoke

SECOND CONJUGATION

vendei	I sold
vendesti	you (fam. sing.) sold

* *Partire* is one of the verbs conjugated with *essere.*

vendè	he (she, it) sold; you (polite sing.) sold
vendemmo	we sold
vendeste	you (fam. pl., also sing.) sold
venderono	they sold; you (polite pl.) sold

THIRD CONJUGATION

partii	I departed
partisti	you (fam. sing.) departed
partì	he (she, it) departed; you (polite sing.) departed
partimmo	we departed
partiste	you (fam. pl., also sing.) departed
partirono	they departed; you (polite pl.) departed

Observations on the Past Definite of the Model Verbs:

You have probably noticed that the characteristic conjugation vowel (*a* for verbs ending in -*are*; *e* for verbs ending in -*ere*; *i* for verbs ending in -*ire*) appears in every form of the past definite, except in the third person singular of the first conjugation verbs (parl*ò*). Aside from the conjugation vowel, the endings in the three conjugations are identical (parl*aste*, vend*este*, part*iste*).

The Past Definite of Irregular Verbs

We have said that many Italian verbs are irregular in the past definite tense. However, there is a definite pattern in their irregularity: (1) three forms of the irregular past definites are always regular (second person singular, first person plural, second person plural); (2) the three irregular forms (first person singular, third person singular, third person plural) always have the same irregular root. Here is the Past Definite of *rispondere* (to answer):

*risposi	I answered
rispondesti	you (fam. sing.) answered
*rispose	he (she, it) answered; you (polite sing.) answered
rispondemmo	we answered

| rispondeste | you (fam. pl., also sing.) answered |
| *risposero | they answered; you (polite pl.) answered |

The starred forms are irregular, but since they always follow the same pattern, you need memorize only the first person singular (*risposi*) and change the -*i* to -*e* and -*ero* to get the other two irregular persons (the third person singular and the third person plural).

Common Irregular Past Definites

avere (to have)	ebbi (I had)
nascere (to be born)	nacqui (I was born)
scrivere (to write)	scrissi (I wrote)
leggere (to read)	lessi (I read)
rispondere (to answer)	risposi (I answered)
venire (to come)	venni (I came)
conoscere (to know)	conobbi (I knew)
scendere (to go down)	scesi (I went down)
chiudere (to close)	chiusi (I closed)
chiedere (to ask)	chiesi (I asked)
*fare (to do, to make)	feci (I did)
*dire (to say)	dissi (I said)

The Past Definite of *Essere* and *Dare*

These two verbs contain irregularities which are not covered in the preceding section and must therefore be memorized in their entirety.

Essere

fui	I was
fosti	you (fam. sing.) were
fu	he (she, it) was; you (polite sing.) were
fummo	we were
foste	you (fam. pl., also sing.) were
furono	they were; you (polite pl.) were

* The original infinitives of *fare* and *dire* (*facere* and *dicere*) are used in the past definite tense. We therefore have: *facesti, facemmo, faceste; dicesti, dicemmo, diceste*. Some less commonly used verbs follow a similar pattern.

Dare

diedi	I gave
desti	you (fam. sing.) gave
diede	he (she, it) gave; you (polite sing.) gave
demmo	we gave
deste	you (fam. pl., also sing.) gave
diedero	they gave; you (polite pl.) gave

The Imperfect Tense

The imperfect tense is used to tell what was happening or what used to happen in the past. It is also the tense of description in the past. It is extremely simple to conjugate a verb in the imperfect tense, since all verbs with the exception of *essere* form their imperfect in the same way. The endings of the three conjugations are identical, but each conjugation keeps its characteristic vowel.

The Imperfect Tense of the Model Verbs

FIRST CONJUGATION

parlavo	I spoke, used to speak, was speaking
parlavi	you (fam. sing.) spoke, used to speak, were speaking
parlava	he (she, it) spoke, used to speak, was speaking; you (polite sing.) spoke, used to speak, were speaking
parlavamo	we spoke, used to speak, were speaking
parlavate	you (fam. pl., also sing.) spoke, used to speak, were speaking
parlavano	they spoke, used to speak, were speaking; you (polite pl.) spoke, used to speak, were speaking

SECOND CONJUGATION

vendevo	I sold, used to sell, was selling
vendevi	you (fam. sing.) sold, used to sell, were selling

vendeva	he (she, it) sold, used to sell, was selling; you (polite sing.) sold, used to sell, were selling
vendevamo	we sold, used to sell, were selling
vendevate	you (fam. pl., also sing.) sold, used to sell, were selling
vendevano	they sold, used to sell, were selling; you (polite pl.) sold, used to sell, were selling

THIRD CONJUGATION

partivo	I departed, used to depart, was departing
partivi	you (fam. sing.) departed, used to depart, were departing
partiva	he (she, it) departed, used to depart, was departing; you (polite sing.) departed, used to depart, were departing
partivamo	we departed, used to depart, were departing
partivate	you (fam. pl., also sing.) departed, used to depart, were departing
partivano	they departed, used to depart, were departing; you (polite pl.) departed, used to depart, were departing

The Imperfect Tense of *Essere*

ero	I was, used to be
eri	you (fam. sing.) were, used to be
era	he (she, it) was, used to be; you (polite sing.) were, used to be
eravamo	we were, used to be
eravate	you (fam. pl., also sing.) were, used to be
erano	they were, used to be; you (polite pl.) were, used to be

The Uses of the Imperfect Tense

The following sentences illustrate the differences in use between the imperfect and the present perfect and the past definite tenses.

Generally speaking, the *imperfect* is the tense used to describe something in the past, or to refer to something which used to happen or was happening in the past. The *present perfect* and the *past definite* both refer to a single completed action which happened at some definite time in the past.

Lo *vedevo* ogni giorno. (Him I used to see every day.)	I *used to see* him every day.
Lo *vidi* ieri. (Him I saw yesterday.)	I *saw* him yesterday.
L'*ho visto* stamani. (Him I have seen this morning.)	I *saw* him this morning.
Leggevo quando *suonò* il campanello.	I *was reading* when he *rang* the bell.
Dove *andavi* quando ti *ho visto?* (Where you were going when you I have seen?)	Where *were* you *going* when I *saw* you?
Quando *eravamo* bambini *giocavamo* tutto il giorno.	When we *were* children, we *used to play* all day.

Verbs which by their very nature express an attitude or a condition, a state of being or a state of mind, rather than an action, are those most frequently used in the imperfect. Here are some of the important ones:

volere (to want)	sperare (to hope)
credere (to think, believe)	sapere (to know)
potere (to be able)	essere (to be)

Non *sapevo* se sarebbero venuti. (Not I knew if they would have come.)	I *didn't know* whether they would come.
Eravamo in quattro. (We were in four.)	There *were* four of us.

Volevo vederla.   I *wanted* to see her.

Non *avevamo* denaro.   We *had* no money.

The Pluperfect Tense

The pluperfect is a compound tense, like the present perfect. But instead of being formed with the present tense of the helping verb and the past participle, it is formed with the *imperfect tense* of the helping verb and the past participle. It is used, as in English, to refer to an action which *had* taken place prior to another action in the past. The helping verb is either *avere* or *essere*, according to the rule discussed on page 63.

The Pluperfect Tense of the Model Verbs

FIRST CONJUGATION

avevo parlato	I had spoken
avevi parlato	you (fam. sing.) had spoken
aveva parlato	he (she, it) had spoken; you (polite sing.) had spoken
avevamo parlato	we had spoken
avevate parlato	you (fam. pl., also sing.) had spoken
avevano parlato	they had spoken; you (polite pl.) had spoken

SECOND CONJUGATION

avevo venduto	I had sold
avevi venduto	you (fam. sing.) had sold
aveva venduto	he (she, it) had sold; you (polite sing.) had sold
avevamo venduto	we had sold
avevate venduto	you (fam. pl., also sing.) had sold
avevano venduto	they had sold; you (polite pl.) had sold

THIRD CONJUGATION

ero partito (-a)	I had departed

eri partito (-a)	you (fam. sing.) had departed
era partito (-a)	he (she, it) had departed; you (polite sing.) had departed
eravamo partiti (-e)	we had departed
eravate partiti (-e)	you (fam. pl., also sing.) had departed
eravate partito (-a)	
erano partiti (-e)	they had departed; you (polite pl.) had departed

Use of the Pluperfect Tense

Non *ero* mai *stato* in Italia.   I *had* never *been* in Italy.
Gli *avevo scritto* prima di partire.   I *had written* him before leaving.

For the sake of completeness, we must mention that there is a *second pluperfect tense* in Italian, formed with the past definite tense of the helping verb and the past participle: *ebbi visto* (I had seen), *avesti visto* (you had seen), etc.   This tense is used in a dependent clause.   But as a beginning student you should avoid long, complicated sentences.   You will therefore have little use for this second tense.

The Future Tense

The future tense (in English, *will* or *shall* plus the infinitive: "I shall go") is formed by dropping the final *-e* of the infinitive and adding the endings *-ò*, *-ai*, *-à*, *-emo*, *-ete*, *-anno*.   In verbs of the first conjugation the *a* of the infinitive changes to *e* (cantare (to sing), canterò (I shall sing)).

The Future Tense of the Model Verbs

FIRST CONJUGATION

parlerò	I shall speak
parlerai	you (fam. sing.) will speak
parlerà	he (she, it) will speak; you (polite sing.) will speak
parleremo	we shall speak
parlerete	you (fam. pl., also sing.) will speak
parleranno	they will speak; you (polite pl.) will speak

SECOND CONJUGATION

venderò	I shall sell
venderai	you (fam. sing.) will sell
venderà	he (she, it) will sell; you (polite sing.) will sell
venderemo	we shall sell
venderete	you (fam. pl., also sing.) will sell
venderanno	they will sell; you (polite pl.) will sell

THIRD CONJUGATION

partirò	I shall leave
partirai	you (fam. sing.) will leave
partirà	he (she, it) will leave; you (polite sing.) will leave
partiremo	we shall leave
partirete	you (fam. pl., also sing.) will leave
partiranno	they will leave; you (polite pl.) will leave

The Future Tense of Irregular Verbs

VERBS IN WHICH THE CONJUGATION VOWEL IS DROPPED

A number of common verbs are irregular in the future because the conjugation vowel (and*are*, av*ere*) is dropped before the future endings are added.

andare (to go)	andrò, andrai, andrà, andremo, andrete, andranno
avere (to have)	avrò, avrai, avrà, avremo, avrete, avranno
potere (to be able)	potrò, potrai, potrà, potremo, potrete, potranno
sapere (to know)	saprò, saprai, saprà, sapremo, saprete, sapranno
dovere (to have to)	dovrò, dovrai, dovrà, dovremo, dovrete, dovranno

vivere (to live)   vivrò, vivrai, vivrà, vivremo, vivrete, vivranno

vedere (to see)   vedrò, vedrai, vedrà, vedremo, vedrete, vedranno

VERBS IN WHICH THE CONJUGATION VOWEL IS DROPPED AND THE PRECEDING CONSONANT BECOMES "R"

In a number of common verbs, the dropping of the conjugation vowel brings with it an additional change before the future endings are added.

tenere (to hold)   terrò, terrai, terrà, terremo, terrete, terranno

rimanere (to remain)   rimarrò, rimarrai, rimarrà, rimarremo, rimarrete, rimarranno

volere (to want)   vorrò, vorrai, vorrà, vorremo, vorrete, vorranno

venire (to come)   verrò, verrai, verrà, verremo, verrete, verranno

THE FUTURE TENSE OF "ESSERE"

sarò	I shall be
sarai	you (fam. sing.) will be
sarà	he (she, it) will be; you (polite sing.) will be
saremo	we shall be
sarete	you (fam. pl., also sing.) will be
saranno	they will be; you (polite pl.) will be

The Uses of the Future Tense

Study the following sentences which illustrate the use of the future in Italian.   In general, English and Italian use corresponds.

Che cosa farà domani sera?   What *will* you *do* tomorrow evening?

Credo che *andremo* a visitare degli amici.	I think that we *shall go* to visit some friends.
Ritorneremo presto però.	We *shall return* early, however.
Quando *partirete?*	When *will* you *leave?*

There is one use of the future in Italian which has no equivalent in English. The future is used in Italian to express what is probable in the present.

Saranno le tre. (They will be the three.)	It *is probably* three o'clock.
Sarà il presidente che parla.	It *is probably* the president who is speaking.

In Italian, there is also a *future perfect tense*, formed with the future tense of the helping verb and the past participle. This tense is used to refer to an action that will have taken place before another action in the future. In English, the present perfect is frequently used instead of the future perfect tense.

Quando *avrò scritto* la lettera, l'imposterò. (When I *shall have written* the letter, I shall mail it.)	When I *have written* the letter, I shall mail it.

The Conditional Mood

The conditional (in English, *would* plus the infinitive) is formed by taking the stem used in the future and adding the endings *-ei, -esti, -ebbe, -emmo, -este, -ebbero.* Whatever irregularities appear in the future will therefore also appear in the conditional.

The Conditional of the Model Verb *Parlare*

parlerei	I would speak
parleresti	you (fam. sing.) would speak
parlerebbe	he (she, it) would speak; you (polite sing.) would speak

parleremmo — we would speak
parlereste — you (fam. pl., also sing.) would speak
parlerebbero — they would speak; you (polite pl.) would speak

The Conditional of Irregular Verbs

andare (to go) — andrei, andresti, andrebbe, andremmo, andreste, andrebbero

essere (to be) — sarei, saresti, sarebbe, saremmo, sareste, sarebbero

avere (to have) — avrei, avresti, avrebbe, avremmo, avreste, avrebbero

sapere (to know) — saprei, sapresti, saprebbe, sapremmo, sapreste, saprebbero

volere (to want) — vorrei, vorresti, vorrebbe, vorremmo, vorreste, vorrebbero

The Uses of the Conditional

The conditional is used in Italian as it is in English (I *would come*, if I could). It is also used, contrary to English, to express what is reported by hearsay.

Io non lo *farei*. — I *would* not *do* it.

Mi *farebbe* il piacere di aprire la porta? — *Would* you *do* me the favor of opening the door?

Secondo lui, *sarebbe* tempo di andare. — According to him, it *is* time to go.

There is also a *conditional perfect*, formed with the conditional of the helping verb and the past participle. It is used like the corresponding tense in English and also to express what was reported by hearsay.

L'*avrei fatto* con piacere. — I *would have done* it with pleasure.

Secondo lui, *sarebbe stato* tempo di andare. — According to him, it *was* time to go.

A further discussion of the conditional in if-sentences will be found on pages 80 and 81.

The Subjunctive Mood

The subjunctive, which survives in English in sentences such as "If I *were* to tell you, you wouldn't believe me," occurs much more frequently in Italian. It is therefore important that you know something about it and that you be familiar with its forms. With very few exceptions, the subjunctive occurs only in dependent clauses. Although it is usually possible to break up a long, complex sentence into two or more short, simple sentences, there are cases where this is impossible. Instead of saying, "Here is the girl whom we met yesterday," we can very well say, "Here is the girl. We met her yesterday." But how else can we express ideas such as, "I want you to open the window" or "I would come if I could," except in the way just stated? We shall limit our explanation of the uses of the subjunctive to these two situations and just a few others.

Tenses of the Subjunctive

THE PRESENT SUBJUNCTIVE OF THE MODEL VERB "PARLARE"

che io parli	that I speak
che tu parli	that you (fam. sing.) speak
che egli (Lei) parli	that he (you) speak
che noi parliamo	that we speak
che voi parliate	that you (fam. pl., also sing.) speak
che essi (Loro) parlino	that they (you) speak

THE PRESENT PERFECT SUBJUNCTIVE OF THE MODEL VERB "PARLARE"

che io abbia parlato	that I have spoken
che tu abbia parlato	that you (fam. sing.) have spoken
che egli (Lei) abbia parlato	that he (you) have spoken
che noi abbiamo parlato	that we have spoken

che voi abbiate parlato	that you (fam. pl., also sing.) have spoken
che essi (Loro) abbiano parlato	that they (you) have spoken

THE PAST SUBJUNCTIVE OF THE MODEL VERB "PARLARE"

che io parlassi	that I spoke
che tu parlassi	that you (fam sing.) spoke
che egli (Lei) parlasse	that he (you) spoke
che noi parlassimo	that we spoke
che voi parlaste	that you (fam. pl., also sing.) spoke
che essi (Loro) parlassero	that they (you) spoke

THE PAST PERFECT SUBJUNCTIVE OF THE MODEL VERB "PARLARE"

che io avessi parlato	that I had spoken
che tu avessi parlato	that you (fam. sing.) had spoken
che egli (Lei) avesse parlato	that he (you) had spoken
che noi avessimo parlato	that we had spoken
che voi aveste parlato	that you (fam. pl., also sing.) had spoken
che essi (Loro) avessero parlato	that they (you) had spoken

The Present and Past Subjunctive of the Model Verbs *vendere* and *partire*:

THE PRESENT SUBJUNCTIVE

che io venda	che io parta
che tu venda	che tu parta
che egli (Lei) venda	che egli (Lei) parta
che noi vendiamo	che noi partiamo
che voi vendiate	che voi partiate
che essi (Loro) vendano	che essi (Loro) partano

THE PAST SUBJUNCTIVE

che io vendessi	che io partissi

che tu vendessi	che tu partissi
che egli (Lei) vendesse	che egli (Lei) partisse
che noi vendessimo	che noi partissimo
che voi vendeste	che voi partiste
che essi (Loro) vendessero	che essi (Loro) partissero

Observations on the Subjunctive Forms of Regular Verbs:

1. In the present subjunctive the first, second, and third persons singular are identical in each conjugation.

2. The first person plural of the present subjunctive is the same as the first person plural of the present indicative.

3. In the second and third conjugations, the endings are identical.

4. Whatever vowel appears in the ending of the singular forms of the present subjunctive is also used in the third person plural (canti, cantino; venda, vendano).

5. In the past subjunctive the endings are identical for the three conjugations, except that each conjugation keeps its conjugation vowel (parlassi, vendessi, partissi).

6. The past subjunctive of all verbs, just like the imperfect, is regular. The only exception is *essere* (fossi, fossi, fosse, fossimo, foste, fossero).

7. The present perfect subjunctive and the past perfect subjunctive are formed respectively with the present subjunctive and the past subjunctive of the helping verb plus the past participle.

The Present Subjunctive of Irregular Verbs

Many verbs which are irregular in the present indicative are also irregular in the present subjunctive. Here is a list of the most common:

INFINITIVE	PRESENT INDICATIVE	PRESENT SUBJUNCTIVE
fare	faccio	faccia, facciamo, facciate, facciano
andare	vado	vada, andiamo, andiate, vadano

volere	voglio	voglia, vogliamo, vogliate, vogliano
venire	vengo	venga, veniamo, veniate, vengano
bere	bevo	beva, beviamo, beviate, bevano
potere	posso	possa, possiamo, possiate, possano
avere	ho	abbia, abbiamo, abbiate, abbiano
essere	sono	sia, siamo, siate, siano

This is an excellent opportunity to review irregular verbs. Turn back to page 58 and go through the whole list, reciting the present indicative and the present subjunctive for each verb.

The Uses of the Subjunctive

The subjunctive is commonly used in the following situations:

1. After a verb of desiring in the main clause of a sentence, the subjunctive is used in the dependent clause when the dependent clause has a different subject.

Voglio che tu *apra* la porta.   I want you to open the door.
(I want that you *open* the door.)

(Compare: *Voglio aprire la porta*, I want to open the door [that is, myself].)

2. After verbs of doubt:

Non so se egli *venga*.   I don't know if he *is coming*.

3. After many impersonal verbs:

È necessario che loro *partano*.   It is necessary that they leave.

Mi sembra che tu *abbia* ragione.   It seems to me that you *are* right.

Mi piace che Lei *sia venuto*.   I am pleased that you *have come*.

4. To express a wish:

Viva la libertà!   (Long) *live* freedom!

5. In "contrary-to-fact" if-sentences:

(referring to the present:)

Se *fossi* più giovane, la sposerei.   If I *were* younger [but I'm not], I'd marry her.

(referring to the past:)

Se *fossi stato* più giovane, l'avrei sposata.   If I *had been younger* [but I wasn't], I'd have married her.

NOTE: In these "contrary-to-fact" if-sentences, in which the if's cannot be fulfilled, the past subjunctive is normally used in the if-clause and the conditional in the main clause, when the present is referred to (if I were younger *now*). When referring to the past (what might have been), use the past perfect subjunctive in the if-clause and the conditional perfect in the main clause. (A simple if-sentence, with possibility of fulfillment, does not require the subjunctive: *Se posso, verrò,* If I can, I'll come.)

Reflexive Verbs

Comparison of Reflexive Verbs in English and Italian

In English, we say: "I get up," "I wash," "I shave," "I dress." In each case the action of the verb refers back to the subject. We might also say: "I wash myself," "I shave myself," "I dress myself." This is what is done in Italian where the reflexive pronoun (*mi, ti, si, ci, vi, si*) must be used with all reflexive verbs. In Italian, the reflexive pronoun precedes the verb, except in those cases where, like the object pronoun, it follows the verb and is written as one word with it (see page 43).

The Present Tense of Reflexive Verbs

guardarsi (to look at oneself): Note that the reflexive pronoun *si* is added to the infinitive after the final *e* has been dropped.

mi guardo   I look at myself
ti guardi   you (fam. sing.) look at yourself
si guarda   he (she, it) looks at himself (herself, itself); you (polite sing.) look at yourself

ci guardiamo	we look at ourselves
vi guardate	you (fam. pl., also sing.) look at yourself (yourselves)
si guardano	they look at themselves; you (polite pl.) look at yourselves

The Present Perfect Tense of Reflexive Verbs

Note that reflexive verbs are all conjugated with *essere* and that the past participle agrees with the subject.

mi sono guardato (-a)	I looked at myself
ti sei guardato (-a)	you (fam. sing.) looked at yourself
si è guardato (-a)	he (she, it) looked at himself (herself); you (polite sing.) looked at yourself
ci siamo guardati (-e)	we looked at ourselves
vi siete guardati (-e)	you (fam. pl., also sing.) looked at yourself (yourselves)
vi siete guardato (-a)	
si sono guardati (-e)	they looked at themselves; you (polite pl.) looked at yourselves

The Command Form or Imperative of Reflexive Verbs

guarda*ti*	look (fam. sing.) at yourself
si guardi	look (polite sing.) at yourself
guardiamo*ci*	let us look at one another, at ourselves
guardate*vi*	look (fam. pl., also sing.) at yourself (yourselves)
si guardino	look (polite pl.) at yourselves

Important Reflexive Verbs

Reflexive verbs are more frequent in Italian than in English. *Alzarsi* (to get up), *sedersi* (to sit down), *vestirsi* (to get dressed), for instance, are reflexive in Italian while they are not in English.

divertirsi	to have a good time
coricarsi	to lie down

svegliarsi	to wake up
sentirsi bene (or male)	to feel well (or ill)
sposarsi	to get married
farsi la barba	to shave
togliersi	to take off (as clothing)
avvicinarsi	to come closer
riposarsi	to rest

Uses of the Reflexive

The following sentences illustrate reflexive and non-reflexive uses of verbs. Study them carefully.

Mia zia è vecchia. Non *sente* bene.	My aunt is old. She doesn't *hear* well.
Ho un raffreddore. Non *mi sento* bene.	I have a cold. I don't *feel* well.
Scrivo spesso ai miei amici.	I often *write* my friends.
Ci scriviamo spesso.	We often *write to one another*.
Ho svegliato mio fratello.	I *woke up* my brother.
Si è svegliato tardi stamani.	He *woke up* late this morning.
Chiama la guardia.	*Call* the police officer.
Mi chiamo Carlo.	*I am called* Charles.
(Myself I call Charles.)	

The reflexive is often used to avoid use of the possessive adjective with parts of the body or with articles of clothing. Observe the following examples:

Mi metto le scarpe.	I am putting on my shoes.
Mi lavo le mani.	I wash my hands.

In Italian, the reflexive is also used where English uses an impersonal construction such as "Here one speaks English," or "They say it is so," or "We do it that way," or where in English the passive would be used: "This is how it is said."

Qui *si parla* inglese.	Here one speaks English.

Come *si dice* "pencil" in italiano?	How do you say "pencil" in Italian?
Si va al cinema?	Are we going to the movies?
Si fa così.	It is done this way.
Si fanno molte cose.	Many things are done.
Si deve comprare il biglietto prima d'entrare.	You must buy the ticket before entering.

The Passive Voice

In Italian, the passive is formed as it is in English, by using the verb "to be" (*essere*) with the past participle: "The book *was written* by Mr. Jones." The reflexive construction, discussed above, is often used instead of the passive in Italian. However, when the person doing the action is mentioned, it is impossible to use the reflexive and the passive must be used. The following examples will make this point clear:

Questa lettera *fu scritta** dalla segretaria.	This letter *was written* by the secretary.
Si scrivono molte lettere in un anno.	Many letters *are written* in a year.
Questo palazzo *fu costruito* da un architetto famoso.	This building *was built* by a famous architect.
Si sono costruiti molti palazzi nuovi.	Many new buildings *have been built*.

Prepositions and Infinitives

Verbs Followed Directly by the Infinitive

As in English ("I must go home"), many common Italian verbs are followed directly by the infinitive without an intervening preposition. Study these examples:

Vuole andare al cinema?	Do you want to go to the movies?

---

* Note that the past participle agrees with the subject, as it always does when the verb is conjugated with *essere*.

Devo partire domani mattina.	I must leave tomorrow morning.
Dobbiamo uscire presto.	We must go out early.
Faccia chiudere la finestra.	Have the window closed.
Mi *potrebbe* prestare del denaro?	Could you lend me some money?
Le *piace* ballare?	Do you like to dance?

As is apparent from the last example, there are many cases where in English you will find the infinitive preceded by "to" while no preposition is used in Italian.

Verbs Followed by *a* or *di* before the Infinitive

Study the following sentences:

Impariamo *a* leggere e scrivere.	We are learning to read and write.
M'insegna *a* nuotare.	He is teaching me to swim.
Cominciamo *a* capire meglio.	We are beginning to understand better.
Mi aiuti *a* chiudere la finestra.	Help me to close the window.
Ho deciso *di* partire.	I decided to leave.
Gli ho domandato *di* portarmelo.	I asked him to bring it to me.
Le dico *di* non disturbarmi.	I tell you not to bother me.
Ha dimenticato *di* farlo.	He forgot to do it.

Only repeated use will help you to remember which verbs are followed by *di*, which by *a*, and which take no preposition at all. For the beginning student it is sufficient to remember the examples given.

The Present Participle and the Infinitive

In English, the present participle is used after prepositions (before *leaving*, after *eating*, without *thinking*). In Italian, it is never so used, but the infinitive is used instead.

prima di *partire*	before leaving
senza *parlare*	without speaking
all'*entrare*	upon entering
*dopo *essere arrivati*	after arriving (after having arrived)

Prima di partire dobbiamo pagare il conto.	*Before leaving* we must pay the bill.
Se ne andò *senza parlare*.	He left *without speaking*.
All'entrare dell'attrice, il pubblico si è alzato.	*Upon* the actress's *entering*, the audience rose.
Dopo essere arrivati, si misero a sedere.	*After arriving*, they sat down.

Idiomatic Constructions

We have seen that there are many parallel constructions in English and Italian. But there are also many idiomatic expressions in Italian which have no exact parallel in English. These cannot be translated literally, nor can they always be explained grammatically or logically. It is important to learn most of these expressions because without them you would be unable to say many of the common things you are most anxious to say.

The Verb *Piacere*

The English verb "to like" is translated by the Italian verb *piacere* (to please). In English you say, "I like Rome," or "I like Rome and Florence," but in Italian you must turn the sentence around to read, "Rome is pleasing to me," or "Rome and Florence are pleasing to me." *Piacere* is therefore used most frequently in the third person, singular and plural, and what is the subject in English becomes an indirect object pronoun in Italian.

---

* Note that after *dopo* the compound infinitive (the infinitive of the helping verb and the past participle) must be used.

mi			I like
ti			you (fam. sing.) like
gli	piace (it is pleasing)		he likes
le			she likes
Le	piacciono (they are pleasing)		you (polite sing.) like
ci			we like
vi			you (fam. pl.) like

piace (piacciono) loro — they like

piace (piacciono) Loro — you (polite pl.) like

Study the following sentences:

Mi piace ballare.	I like to dance. (To me it is pleasing to dance.)
Le piacciono questi fiori?	Do you like these flowers? (To you are pleasing these flowers?)
Ci è piaciuto il film ieri sera.	We liked the movie last night. (To us was pleasing the film yesterday evening.)
Gli piacciono molto.	He likes them very much. (To him they are pleasing very much.)
Mi sono piaciuti i fiori.	I liked the flowers. (To me were pleasing the flowers.)
Piace viaggiare a tua sorella?	Does your sister like to travel? (Is it pleasing to travel for your sister?)

Observe that *piacere* is conjugated with *essere* and that the past participle therefore agrees with the subject (the object in English).

The Verb *Fare*

Fare (to do, to make) is used in a variety of idiomatic expressions, where English uses other verbs.

1. Expressions of weather:

Che tempo *fa*?	How is the weather? (What weather *makes* it?)
Fa bel (cattivo) tempo.	The weather is fine (bad). (It *makes* good (bad) weather.)
Fa freddo.	It is cold. (It *makes* cold.)
Fa molto caldo.	It is very hot. (It *makes* very hot.)
Note however:	
Piove.	It is raining.
Tira vento.	The wind is blowing.

2. Professions:

Che cosa *fa* Suo padre?	What does your father *do*?
Mio padre *fa* il medico.	My father is a doctor. (He exercises the profession of doctor.)
Faccio il musicista.	I am a musician.

3. *Fare* used in place of English "have":

Faccia aprire la porta.	Have the door opened.
Mi *son fatto* fare un vestito.	I had a dress made for myself.
Le *ho fatto* scrivere una lettera.	I had her write a letter (or, I had a letter written to her).

Note that in Italian the *infinitive* and not the past participle is used in this construction.

4. Other idiomatic uses:

fare una domanda	to ask a question
fare un viaggio	to take a trip
fare un bagno	to take a bath
fare una passeggiata	to take a walk
fare colazione	to have breakfast or lunch
fare da mangiare	to prepare lunch or dinner
fare attenzione	to pay attention

fare un piacere	to do a favor
fare una conferenza	to give a lecture
farsi male	to hurt oneself
farsi ricco	to become rich
farsi la barba	to shave
Si *fa* tardi.	It is getting late.
Non *fa* niente.	It's all right.

The Verb *Avere*

"To be hungry, thirsty, warm, etc.," are rendered in Italian by the verb *avere* with the noun: "to have hunger, thirst, etc."

Ho fame.	I am hungry.
Ho sete.	I am thirsty.
Ho caldo.	I am warm.
Ho freddo.	I am cold.
Ho fretta.	I am in a hurry.
Ho paura.	I am afraid.
Hai ragione.	You (fam. sing.) are right.
Ho sonno.	I am sleepy.

Observe also:

Ho venticinque anni.	I am twenty-five years old.
Ha i capelli biondi e gli occhi azzurri.	His hair is blond and his eyes are blue.
Che cos'*hai*?	What is the matter with you (fam. sing.)?
Non *ho* niente.	Nothing is the matter with me.

The Verbs *Essere* and *Stare*

Although *essere* and *stare* both mean "to be," they are not interchangeable. In English, "to be" expresses many different ideas: "Rome and Florence *are* in Italy" (i.e., are located); "Two and two *are* four" (i.e., equal four); "We are sick" (i.e., condition); "We *are* going home" (part of the progressive). In Italian, *essere* is used as a helping verb; *stare* is used to form the progressive. *Stare* is the verb used to refer to health in phrases such as *Sto bene*

(I'm well) and *Come sta?* (How are you?). Study the following examples which illustrate the different uses of *essere* and *stare*:

Roma e Firenze *sono* in Italia.	Rome and Florence are in Italy.
Siamo ammalati.	We are ill.
Siamo arrivati.	We arrived.
Stiamo andando a casa.	We are going home.
Stiamo a Milano.	We live in Milan.
Stiamo bene.	We are well.
Come *sta?*	How are you (polite sing.)?
Stiamo per andare a casa.	We are about to go home.
Le piace *stare* in piedi?	Do you like to stand up?
Stia zitto!	Be (polite sing.) quiet!
Stai a sentire!	Just listen (fam. sing.) to this!

C'è and *Ci sono*

C'è means "there is"; *ci sono*, "there are"; *c'era*, "there was"; *c'erano*, "there were."

C'è ancora molto da fare.	*There is* still much to do.
Ci sono quattro posti liberi.	*There are* four empty places.
C'era molto da vedere.	*There was* much to be seen.
C'erano molte cose da vedere.	*There were* many things to be seen.

Aver bisogno and *Bisognare*

Confusion between these two expressions arises because of their similarity. *Aver bisogno di* is used to express a lack of something and translated literally as "to have need of." The impersonal verb *bisognare*, instead, means "to be necessary" and is followed by the subjunctive. Study these sentences:

Ho bisogno di un paio di scarpe.	*I need* a pair of shoes.
Bisogna ch'egli parta.	*It is necessary* that he go.

The Verb *Volere*

Volere (to wish, to want) has a variety of uses:

Voglio partire subito.	*I want* to leave at once.
Vuol farmi questo favore?	*Will* you do me this favor?
Vorrei andarci anch'io.	I, too, *would like* to go there.
Cosa *vuol* dire questa parola?	What does this word mean?
Ci *vogliono* due ore per andare da Bologna a Firenze.	It *takes* two hours to go from Bologna to Florence.
Come *vuole*.	As you *wish*.
Voglio bene a mia madre.	I love my mother.

The Verbs *Dare* and *Andare*

Some idioms with *dare*:

dar ragione, *dar* torto	to agree, to disagree
dare la mano a	to shake hands with
dare del tu, del voi, del Lei	to use *tu, voi, Lei* in direct address

Some idioms with *andare*:

andare in automobile, in treno	to go by car, by train
andare a cavallo	to ride horseback
Come *va*?	How goes it?
Va bene.	Very well.

The Verbs *Sapere* and *Conoscere*

Although both *sapere* and *conoscere* are translated by "to know," they are not interchangeable. Essentially, *sapere* means "to know" in the sense of "to have knowledge"; *conoscere*, in the sense of "to be acquainted with." *Conoscere* may also be used in the sense of "to meet," "to make the acquaintance of."

Sa che ora è?	Do you *know* what time it is?
Conosco quel signore.	I *know* that gentleman.
Vorrei *conoscerlo*.	I'd like to *meet* him.
Non *sa* suonare il pianoforte.	He doesn't *know how* to play the piano.
Piacere di *conoscerLa*!	Pleased to *meet* you!
So dov'è la stazione.	I *know* where the station is.
Conosco quell'albergo.	I *know* that hotel.

Some Useful Expressions

Study these useful expressions which have not appeared in the main body of this book.

Che ore sono?	What time is it? (LIT. What hours are?)
Che ora è?	What time is it? (LIT. What hour is?)
Sono le otto e mezza.	It is half-past eight.
È mezzogiorno.	It is noon.
Mi mancano i miei.	I miss my family.
Non importa.	It doesn't matter.
Non ci pensi.	Don't worry about it.
Mi dispiace.	I'm sorry.
Peccato!	Too bad! What a pity!
Va bene.	All right.
Lei è molto gentile.	You are very kind.
Si diverta!	Have a good time!
Buon appetito!	Enjoy your meal!
Davvero!	Really! You don't say so!
Non va.	It's no good.
Buon giorno.	Good morning.
Buona sera.	Good evening.
Buona notte.	Good night.
Arrivederci.	So long.
Arrivederci a domani.	So long until tomorrow.
A domani.	See you tomorrow.
Dopo pranzo.	In the afternoon. (After lunch.)
Dopodomani.	The day after tomorrow.
Ieri l'altro.	The day before yesterday.
Subito.	At once.
Fra poco.	In a little while.

Finalmente.	Finally. At last.
Di nuovo.	Again.
Invece.	Instead.
Bene.	Well. Good.
Forse.	Perhaps.
Quindi.	Therefore.
Almeno.	At least.
S'intende.	Of course.
Certo.	Certainly.
Come no!	Naturally!
Tutti.	Everybody.
Tutto.	Everything.
Con piacere.	Willingly. With pleasure.
Molte grazie.	Many thanks.
Prego.	You're welcome.
Scusi.	Excuse me.
Permesso.	With your permission.

A Glossary of Grammatical Terms

E. F. Bleiler

This section is intended to refresh your memory of grammatical terms or to clear up difficulties you may have had in understanding them.   Before you work through the grammar, you should have a reasonably clear idea what the parts of speech and parts of a sentence are.   This is not for reasons of pedantry, but simply because it is easier to talk about grammar if we agree upon terms.   Grammatical terminology is as necessary to the study of grammar as the names of automobile parts are to garagemen.

This list is not exhaustive, and the definitions do not pretend to be complete, or to settle points of interpretation that grammarians have been disputing for the past several hundred years.   It is a working analysis rather than a scholarly investigation.   The definitions given, however, represent most typical American usage, and should serve for basic use.

The Parts of Speech

English words can be divided into eight important groups: nouns, adjectives, articles, verbs, adverbs, pronouns, prepositions, and conjunctions.   The boundaries between one group of words and another are sometimes vague and ill-felt in English, but a good dictionary, like the *Webster Collegiate*, can help you make decisions in questionable cases.   Always bear in mind, however, that the way a word is used in a sentence may be just as important as the nature of the word itself in deciding what part of speech the word is.

Nouns.   *Nouns* are the *words* for *things* of all *sorts*, whether these *things* are real *objects* that you can see, or *ideas*, or *places*, or *qualities*, or *groups*, or more abstract *things*.   *Examples* of *words* that are *nouns* are *cat, vase, door, shrub, wheat, university, mercy, intelligence, ocean, plumber, pleasure, society, army.* If you are in *doubt* whether a given *word* is a *noun,* try putting the *word* "my," or "this," or "large" (or some other *adjective*) in *front* of it. If it makes *sense* in the *sentence* the *chances* are that the *word* in *question* is a *noun.* [All the *words* in *italics* in this *paragraph* are *nouns.*]

Adjectives. Adjectives are the words which delimit or give you *specific* information about the *various* nouns in a sentence. They tell you size, color, weight, pleasantness, and many *other* qualities. *Such* words as *big, expensive, terrible, insipid, hot, delightful, ruddy, informative* are all *clear* adjectives. If you are in *any* doubt whether a *certain* word is an adjective, add -er to it, or put the word "more" or "too" in front of it. If it makes *good* sense in the sentence, and does not end in -ly, the chances are that it is an adjective. (Pronoun-adjectives will be described under pronouns.) [The adjectives in the *above* sentences are in italics.]

Articles. There are only two kinds of articles in English, and they are easy to remember. The definite article is "the" and the indefinite article is "a" or "an."

Verbs. Verbs *are* the words that *tell* what action, or condition, or relationship *is going* on. Such words as *was, is, jumps, achieved, keeps, buys, sells, has finished, run, will have, may, should pay, indicates are* all verb forms. *Observe* that a verb *can be composed* of more than one word, as *will have* and *should pay,* above; these *are called* compound verbs. As a rough guide for verbs, *try adding* -ed to the word you *are wondering* about, or *taking* off an -ed that *is* already there. If it *makes* sense, the chances *are* that it *is* a verb. (This *does* not always *work,* since the so-called strong or irregular verbs *make* forms by *changing* their middle vowels, like *spring, sprang, sprung.*) [Verbs in this paragraph *are* in italics.]

Adverbs. An adverb is a word that supplies additional information about a verb, an adjective, or another adverb. It *usually* indicates time, or manner, or place, or degree. It tells you

how, or *when*, or *where*, or to what degree things are happening.
Such words as *now, then, there, not, anywhere, never, somehow, always,
very,* and most words ending in -ly are *ordinarily* adverbs.   [Italicized words are adverbs.]

Pronouns.   Pronouns are related to nouns, and take their place.
(Some grammars and dictionaries group pronouns and nouns
together as substantives.)   *They* mention persons, or objects of
any sort without actually giving their names.

There are several different kinds of pronouns.   (1) Personal
pronouns: by a grammatical convention *I, we, me, mine, us, ours*
are called first person pronouns, since *they* refer to the speaker;
you and *yours* are called second person pronouns, since *they* refer
to the person addressed; and *he, him, his, she, hers, they, them,
theirs* are called third person pronouns since *they* refer to the things
or persons discussed.   (2) Demonstrative pronouns: *this, that,
these, those.*   (3) Interrogative, or question, pronouns: *who, whom,
what, whose, which.*   (4) Relative pronouns, or pronouns *which*
refer back to something already mentioned: *who, whom, that,
which.*   (5) Others: *some, any, anyone, no one, other, whichever,
none,* etc.

Pronouns are difficult for *us*, since our categories are not as
clear as in some other languages, and *we* use the same words for
what foreign-language speakers see as different situations.   First,
our interrogative and relative pronouns overlap, and must be
separated in translation.   The easiest way is to observe whether a
question is involved in the sentence.   Examples: "*Which* [int.] do
you like?"   "The inn, *which* [rel.] was not far from Verona, had a
restaurant."   "*Who* [int.] is there?"   "*I* don't know *who* [int.]
was there."   "The porter *who* [rel.] took our bags was Number
2132."   *This* may seem to be a trivial difference to an English
speaker, but in some languages *it* is very important.

Secondly, there is an overlap between pronouns and adjectives.
In some cases the word "this," for example, is a pronoun; in other
cases *it* is an adjective.   *This* also holds true for *his, its, her, any,
none, other, some, that, these, those,* and many other words.   Note

whether the word in question stands alone or is associated with another word. Examples: "*This* [pronoun] is *mine*." "This [adj.] taxi has no springs." Watch out for the word "that," which can be a pronoun or an adjective or a conjunction. And remember that "my," "your," "our," and "their" are always adjectives. [All pronouns in this section are in italics.]

Prepositions. Prepositions are the little words that introduce phrases that tell *about* condition, time, place, manner, association, degree, and similar topics. Such words as *with, in, beside, under, of, to, about, for,* and *upon* are prepositions. In English prepositions and adverbs overlap, but, as you will see *by* checking *in* your dictionary, there are usually differences *of* meaning *between* the two uses. [Prepositions *in* this paragraph are designated *by* italics.]

Conjunctions. Conjunctions are joining-words. They enable you to link words *or* groups of words into larger units, *and* to build compound *or* complex sentences out of simple sentence units. Such words as *and, but, although, or, unless,* are typical conjunctions. *Although* most conjunctions are easy enough to identify, the word "that" should be watched closely to see *that* it is not a pronoun *or* an adjective. [Conjunctions italicized.]

Words about Verbs

Verbs are responsible for most of the terminology in this short grammar. The basic terms are:

Conjugation. In many languages verbs fall into natural groups, according to the way they make their forms. These groupings are called conjugations, and are an aid to learning grammatical structure. Though it may seem difficult at first to speak of First and Second Conjugations, these are simply short ways of saying that verbs belonging to these classes make their forms according to certain consistent rules, which you can memorize.

Infinitive. This is the basic form which most dictionaries give for verbs in most languages, and in most languages it serves as the basis for classifying verbs.   In English (with a very few exceptions) it has no special form.   To find the infinitive for any English verb, just fill in this sentence: "I like to......... (walk, run, jump, swim, carry, disappear, etc.)."   The infinitive in English is usually preceded by the word "to."

Tense.   This is simply a formal way of saying "time."   In English we think of time as being broken into three great segments: past, present, and future.   Our verbs are assigned forms to indicate this division, and are further subdivided for shades of meaning.   We subdivide the present time into the present (I walk) and present progressive (I am walking); the past into the simple past (I walked), progressive past (I was walking), perfect or present perfect (I have walked), past perfect or pluperfect (I had walked); and future into simple future (I shall walk) and future progressive (I shall be walking).   These are the most common English tenses.

Present Participles, Progressive Tenses.   In English the present participle always ends in -*ing*.   It can be used as a noun or an adjective in some situations, but its chief use is in *forming* the so-called progressive tenses.   These are made by *putting* appropriate forms of the verb "to be" before a present participle: For "to walk" [an infinitive], for example, the present progressive would be: I am *walking*, you are *walking*, he is *walking*, etc.; past progressive, I was *walking*, you were *walking*, and so on.   [Present participles are in italics.]

Past Participles, Perfect Tenses.   The past participle in English is not *formed* as regularly as is the present participle. Sometimes it is *constructed* by adding -ed or -d to the present tense, as *walked, jumped, looked, received*; but there are many verbs where it is *formed* less regularly: *seen, been, swum, chosen, brought*.   To find it, simply fill out the sentence "I have........." putting in the verb form that your ear tells you is right for the particular verb.   If you speak grammatically, you will have the past participle.

Past participles are sometimes used as adjectives: "Don't cry over *spilt* milk." Their most important use, however, is to form the system of verb tenses that are *called* the perfect tenses: present perfect (or perfect), past perfect (or pluperfect), etc. In English the present perfect tense is *formed* with the present tense of "to have" and the past participle of a verb: I have *walked*, you have *run*, he has *begun*, etc. The past perfect is *formed*, similarly, with the past tense of "to have" and the past participle: I had *walked*, you had *run*, he had *begun*. Most of the languages you are likely to study have similar systems of perfect tenses, though they may not be *formed* in exactly the same way as in English. [Past participles in italics.]

Preterit, Imperfect. Many languages have more than one verb tense for expressing an action that took place in the past. They may use a perfect tense (which we have just covered), or a preterit, or an imperfect. English, although you may never have thought about it, is one of these languages, for we can say "I have spoken to him" [present perfect], or "I spoke to him" [simple past], or "I was speaking to him" [past progressive]. These sentences do not mean exactly the same thing, although the differences are subtle, and are difficult to put into other words.

While usage differs a little from language to language, if a language has both a preterit and an imperfect, in general the preterit corresponds to the English simple past (I ran, I swam, I spoke), and the imperfect corresponds to the English past progressive (I was running, I was swimming, I was speaking). If you are curious to discover the mode of thought behind these different tenses, try looking at the situation in terms of background-action and point-action. One of the most important uses of the imperfect is to provide a background against which a single point-action can take place. For example, "When I was walking down the street [background, continued over a period of time, hence past progressive or imperfect], I stubbed my toe [an instant or point of time, hence a simple past or preterit]."

Auxiliary Verbs. Auxiliary verbs are special words that are used to help other verbs make their forms. In English, for example, we use forms of the verb "to have" in our perfect tenses: I have seen, you had come, he has been, etc. We also use shall or will to make our future tenses: I shall pay, you will see, etc. French, German, Spanish, and Italian also make use of auxiliary verbs, but although the same general concept is present, the use of auxiliaries differs very much from one language to another, and you must learn the practice for each language.

Reflexive. This term, which sounds more difficult than it really is, simply means that the verb flexes back upon the noun or pronoun that is its subject. In modern English the reflexive pronoun always has -*self* on its end, and we do not use the construction very frequently. In other languages, however, reflexive forms may be used more frequently, and in ways that do not seem very logical to an English speaker. Examples of English reflexive sentences: "He washes himself." "He seated himself at the table."

Passive. In some languages, like Latin, there is a strong feeling that an action or thing that is taking place can be expressed in two different ways. One can say, A does-something-to B, which is "active"; or B is-having-something-done-to-him by A, which is "passive." We do not have a strong feeling for this classification of experience in English, but the following examples should indicate the difference between an active and a passive verb: Active: "John is building a house." Passive: "A house is being built by John." Active: "The steamer carried the cotton to England." Passive: "The cotton was carried by the steamer to England." Bear in mind that the formation of passive verbs and the situations where they can be used vary enormously from language to language. This is one situation where you usually cannot translate English word for word into another language and make sense.

Impersonal Verbs. In English there are some verbs which do not have an ordinary subject, and do not refer to persons. They are always used with the pronoun *it*, which does not refer to anything specifically, but simply serves to fill out the verb forms. Examples: It is snowing. It hailed last night. It seems to me that you are wrong. It has been raining. It won't do.

Other languages, like German, have this same general concept, but impersonal verbs may differ quite a bit in form and frequency from one language to another.

Words about Nouns

Agreement. In some languages, where nouns or adjectives or articles are declined, or have gender endings, it is necessary that the adjective or article be in the same case or gender or number as the noun it goes with (modifies). This is called agreement.

This may be illustrated from Italian, where articles and adjectives have to agree with nouns in gender and number.

una casa rossa	one red house	due case rosse	two red houses
un libro rosso	one red book	due libri rossi	two red books

Here *una* is feminine singular and has the ending -*a* because it agrees with the feminine singular noun *casa*; *rossa* has the ending -*a* because it agrees with the feminine singular noun *casa*. *rosso*, on the other hand, and *un*, are masculine singular because *libro* is masculine singular.

Gender. Gender should not be confused with actual sex. In many languages nouns are arbitrarily assigned a gender (masculine or feminine, or masculine or feminine or neuter), and this need not correspond to sex. You simply have to learn the pattern of the language you are studying in order to become familiar with its use of gender.

Miscellaneous Terms

Comparative, Superlative. These two terms are used with adjectives and adverbs. They indicate the degree of strength within the meaning of the word. Faster, better, earlier, newer, more rapid, more detailed, more suitable are examples of the comparative in adjectives, while more rapidly, more recently, more suitably are comparatives for adverbs. In most cases, as you have seen, the comparative uses -er or "more" for an adjective, and "more" for an adverb. Superlatives are those forms which end in -est or have "most" placed before them for adjectives, and "most" prefixed for adverbs: most intelligent, earliest, most rapidly, most suitably.

Idiom. An idiom is an expression that is peculiar to a language, the meaning of which is not the same as the literal meaning of the individual words composing it. Idioms, as a rule, cannot be translated word by word into another language. Examples of English idioms: "*Take it easy.*" "Don't *beat around the bush.*" "It *turned out* to be *a Dutch treat.*" "Can you *tell time* in Italian?"

The Parts of the Sentence

Subject, Predicate. In grammar *every complete sentence* contains two basic parts, the subject and the predicate. *The subject, if we* state the terms most simply, is the thing, person, or activity talked about. *It* can be a noun, a pronoun, or something *that* serves as a noun. *A subject* would include, in a typical case, a noun, the articles or adjectives *which* are associated with it, and perhaps phrases. Note that in complex sentences, *each part* may have its own subject. [*The subjects of the sentences above* have been italicized.]

The predicate *talks about the subject.* In a formal sentence the predicate *includes a verb, its adverbs, predicate adjectives, phrases, and objects*—whatever *happens to be present.* A predicate adjective *is an adjective* which *happens to be in the predicate after a form of the verb to be.* Example: "Apples *are red.*" [Predicates *are in italics.*]

In the following simple sentences subjects are in italics, predicates in italics and underlined. *"Green apples are bad for your digestion."* *"When I go to Italy, I always stop in Milan."* *"The man with the handbag is travelling to Florence."*

Direct and Indirect Objects. Some verbs (called transitive verbs) take direct and/or indirect objects in their predicates; other verbs (called intransitive verbs) do not take objects of any sort. In English, except for pronouns, objects do not have any special forms, but in languages which have case forms or more pronoun forms than English, objects can be troublesome.

The direct object is the person, thing, quality, or matter that the verb directs *its action* upon. It can be a pronoun, or a noun, perhaps accompanied by an article and/or adjectives. The direct object always directly follows *its verb*, except when there is also an indirect object pronoun present, which comes between the verb and the object. Prepositions do not go before direct objects. Examples: "The cook threw *green onions* into the stew." "The border guards will want to see *your passport* tomorrow." "Give *it* to me." "Please give me *a glass of red wine*." [We have placed *direct objects* in this paragraph in italics.]

The indirect object, as grammars will tell *you*, is the person or thing for or to whom the action is taking place. It can be a pronoun or a noun with or without article and adjectives. In most cases the words "to" or "for" can be inserted before it, if not already there. Examples: "Please tell *me* the time." "I wrote *her* a letter from Rome." "We sent *Mr. Medoni* ten lire." "We gave *the most energetic guide* a large tip." [Indirect objects are in italics.]

Index

The following abbreviations have been used in this index: *adj.* for adjective, *def.* for definition, and *pron.* for pronoun. Italian words appear in *italic* and their English equivalents in parentheses.

negatives 49, 50
non è vero? (isn't it?) 15
nouns 18–24
  def. 94
  feminine forms of masculine
    22, 23
  gender of 18, 21, 22
  plurals of 19–21
    irregular 20, 21
noun suffixes 21

object: *see* direct object, indirect
    object
object pronouns
  direct 42–44
  how to avoid 45
  indirect 42–44
  position of 43
  two with same verb 44, 45
omission of possessive adjective 37

participle: *see* past participle,
    present participle
passive voice 84
  def. 100
  replaced by reflexive construc-
    tion 84
past definite tense 65–68
  compared with imperfect and
    present perfect 70
  of *dare* (to give) 68
  of *essere* (to be) 67
  of irregular verbs 66, 67
  of model verbs 65, 66
past participle 62–64
  def. 98
  in passive voice 84
  irregular 63
past perfect subjunctive 78, 81

past subjunctive 78, 79, 81
perfect tenses
  def. 98
personal pronouns 41–48
  def. 96
  stressed forms of 44
  table of 45–48
piacere (to be pleasing) 86, 87
  conjugated with *essere* 87
pluperfect tense 71, 72
  of model verbs 71, 72
  second 72
  use of 72
plurals of nouns 19–21
  irregular 20, 21
position of adjectives 26, 27
position of object pronouns 43
possession 36, 37
possessive adjectives 36, 37
  replaced by reflexive construc-
    tion 83
  sometimes omitted 37
predicate
  def. 102
prepositions
  before infinitive 85
  contracted with definite article
    23
  def. 97
  pronouns used after 44, 51
present, progressive: *see* progres-
    sive present
present participle 59
  def. 98
  not used after prepositions 85,
    86
present perfect subjunctive 77, 78
present perfect tense 62–65
  compared with imperfect and
    past definite 70

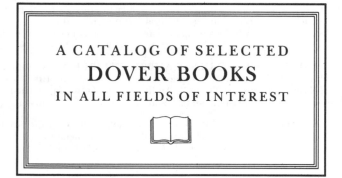

A CATALOG OF SELECTED

DOVER BOOKS

IN ALL FIELDS OF INTEREST

A CATALOG OF SELECTED
DOVER BOOKS
IN ALL FIELDS OF INTEREST

DRAWINGS OF REMBRANDT, edited by Seymour Slive. Updated Lippmann, Hofstede de Groot edition, with definitive scholarly apparatus. All portraits, biblical sketches, landscapes, nudes. Oriental figures, classical studies, together with selection of work by followers. 550 illustrations. Total of 630pp. 9⅛ × 12¼.
21485-0, 21486-9 Pa., Two-vol. set $29.90

GHOST AND HORROR STORIES OF AMBROSE BIERCE, Ambrose Bierce. 24 tales vividly imagined, strangely prophetic, and decades ahead of their time in technical skill: "The Damned Thing," "An Inhabitant of Carcosa," "The Eyes of the Panther," "Moxon's Master," and 20 more. 199pp. 5⅜ × 8½.   20767-6 Pa. $4.95

ETHICAL WRITINGS OF MAIMONIDES, Maimonides. Most significant ethical works of great medieval sage, newly translated for utmost precision, readability. Laws Concerning Character Traits, Eight Chapters, more. 192pp. 5⅜ × 8½.
24522-5 Pa. $5.95

THE EXPLORATION OF THE COLORADO RIVER AND ITS CANYONS, J. W. Powell. Full text of Powell's 1,000-mile expedition down the fabled Colorado in 1869. Superb account of terrain, geology, vegetation, Indians, famine, mutiny, treacherous rapids, mighty canyons, during exploration of last unknown part of continental U.S. 400pp. 5⅜ × 8½.   20094-9 Pa. $8.95

HISTORY OF PHILOSOPHY, Julián Marías. Clearest one-volume history on the market. Every major philosopher and dozens of others, to Existentialism and later. 505pp. 5⅜ × 8½.   21739-6 Pa. $9.95

ALL ABOUT LIGHTNING, Martin A. Uman. Highly readable nontechnical survey of nature and causes of lightning, thunderstorms, ball lightning, St. Elmo's Fire, much more. Illustrated. 192pp. 5⅜ × 8½.   25237-X Pa. $5.95

SAILING ALONE AROUND THE WORLD, Captain Joshua Slocum. First man to sail around the world, alone, in small boat. One of great feats of seamanship told in delightful manner. 67 illustrations. 294pp. 5⅜ × 8½.   20326-3 Pa. $4.95

LETTERS AND NOTES ON THE MANNERS, CUSTOMS AND CONDITIONS OF THE NORTH AMERICAN INDIANS, George Catlin. Classic account of life among Plains Indians: ceremonies, hunt, warfare, etc. 312 plates. 572pp. of text. 6⅛ × 9¼.   22118-0, 22119-9, Pa., Two-vol. set $17.90

THE SECRET LIFE OF SALVADOR DALÍ, Salvador Dalí. Outrageous but fascinating autobiography through Dalí's thirties with scores of drawings and sketches and 80 photographs. A must for lovers of 20th-century art. 432pp. 6½ × 9¼. (Available in U.S. only)   27454-3 Pa. $9.95

ILLUSTRATED DICTIONARY OF HISTORIC ARCHITECTURE, edited by Cyril M. Harris. Extraordinary compendium of clear, concise definitions for over 5,000 important architectural terms complemented by over 2,000 line drawings. Covers full spectrum of architecture from ancient ruins to 20th-century Modernism. Preface. 592pp. 7½ × 9⅝. 24444-X Pa. $15.95

THE NIGHT BEFORE CHRISTMAS, Clement C. Moore. Full text, and woodcuts from original 1848 book. Also critical, historical material. 19 illustrations. 40pp. 4⅝ × 6. 22797-9 Pa. $2.50

THE LESSON OF JAPANESE ARCHITECTURE: 165 Photographs, Jiro Harada. Memorable gallery of 165 photographs taken in the 1930s of exquisite Japanese homes of the well-to-do and historic buildings. 13 line diagrams. 192pp. 8⅜ × 11¼. 24778-3 Pa. $10.95

THE AUTOBIOGRAPHY OF CHARLES DARWIN AND SELECTED LETTERS, edited by Francis Darwin. The fascinating life of eccentric genius composed of an intimate memoir by Darwin (intended for his children); commentary by his son, Francis; hundreds of fragments from notebooks, journals, papers; and letters to and from Lyell, Hooker, Huxley, Wallace and Henslow. xi + 365pp. 5⅜ × 8. 20479-0 Pa. $6.95

WONDERS OF THE SKY: Observing Rainbows, Comets, Eclipses, the Stars and Other Phenomena, Fred Schaaf. Charming, easy-to-read poetic guide to all manner of celestial events visible to the naked eye. Mock suns, glories, Belt of Venus, more. Illustrated. 299pp. 5¼ × 8¼. 24402-4 Pa. $8.95

BURNHAM'S CELESTIAL HANDBOOK, Robert Burnham, Jr. Thorough guide to the stars beyond our solar system. Exhaustive treatment. Alphabetical by constellation: Andromeda to Cetus in Vol. 1; Chamaeleon to Orion in Vol. 2; and Pavo to Vulpecula in Vol. 3. Hundreds of illustrations. Index in Vol. 3. 2,000pp. 6⅛ × 9¼. 23567-X, 23568-8, 23673-0 Pa., Three-vol. set $41.85

STAR NAMES: Their Lore and Meaning, Richard Hinckley Allen. Fascinating history of names various cultures have given to constellations and literary and folkloristic uses that have been made of stars. Indexes to subjects. Arabic and Greek names. Biblical references. Bibliography. 563pp. 5⅜ × 8½. 21079-0 Pa. $9.95

THIRTY YEARS THAT SHOOK PHYSICS: The Story of Quantum Theory, George Gamow. Lucid, accessible introduction to influential theory of energy and matter. Careful explanations of Dirac's anti-particles, Bohr's model of the atom, much more. 12 plates. Numerous drawings. 240pp. 5⅜ × 8½. 24895-X Pa. $6.95

CHINESE DOMESTIC FURNITURE IN PHOTOGRAPHS AND MEASURED DRAWINGS, Gustav Ecke. A rare volume, now affordably priced for antique collectors, furniture buffs and art historians. Detailed review of styles ranging from early Shang to late Ming. Unabridged republication. 161 black-and-white drawings, photos. Total of 224pp. 8⅜ × 11¼. (Available in U.S. only) 25171-3 Pa. $14.95

VINCENT VAN GOGH: A Biography, Julius Meier-Graefe. Dynamic, penetrating study of artist's life, relationship with brother, Theo, painting techniques, travels, more. Readable, engrossing. 160pp. 5⅜ × 8½. (Available in U.S. only) 25253-1 Pa. $4.95

HOW TO WRITE, Gertrude Stein. Gertrude Stein claimed anyone could understand her unconventional writing—here are clues to help. Fascinating improvisations, language experiments, explanations illuminate Stein's craft and the art of writing. Total of 414pp. 4⅜ × 6⅜. 23144-5 Pa. $6.95

ADVENTURES AT SEA IN THE GREAT AGE OF SAIL: Five Firsthand Narratives, edited by Elliot Snow. Rare true accounts of exploration, whaling, shipwreck, fierce natives, trade, shipboard life, more. 33 illustrations. Introduction. 353pp. 5⅜ × 8½. 25177-2 Pa. $9.95

THE HERBAL OR GENERAL HISTORY OF PLANTS, John Gerard. Classic descriptions of about 2,850 plants—with over 2,700 illustrations—includes Latin and English names, physical descriptions, varieties, time and place of growth, more. 2,706 illustrations. xlv + 1,678pp. 8½ × 12¼. 23147-X Cloth. $89.95

DOROTHY AND THE WIZARD IN OZ, L. Frank Baum. Dorothy and the Wizard visit the center of the Earth, where people are vegetables, glass houses grow and Oz characters reappear. Classic sequel to Wizard of Oz. 256pp. 5⅜ × 8. 24714-7 Pa. $5.95

SONGS OF EXPERIENCE: Facsimile Reproduction with 26 Plates in Full Color, William Blake. This facsimile of Blake's original "Illuminated Book" reproduces 26 full-color plates from a rare 1826 edition. Includes "The Tyger," "London," "Holy Thursday," and other immortal poems. 26 color plates. Printed text of poems. 48pp. 5¼ × 7. 24636-1 Pa. $3.95

SONGS OF INNOCENCE, William Blake. The first and most popular of Blake's famous "Illuminated Books," in a facsimile edition reproducing all 31 brightly colored plates. Additional printed text of each poem. 64pp. 5¼ × 7. 22764-2 Pa. $3.95

PRECIOUS STONES, Max Bauer. Classic, thorough study of diamonds, rubies, emeralds, garnets, etc.: physical character, occurrence, properties, use, similar topics. 20 plates, 8 in color. 94 figures. 659pp. 6⅛ × 9¼. 21910-0, 21911-9 Pa., Two-vol. set $21.90

ENCYCLOPEDIA OF VICTORIAN NEEDLEWORK, S. F. A. Caulfeild and Blanche Saward. Full, precise descriptions of stitches, techniques for dozens of needlecrafts—most exhaustive reference of its kind. Over 800 figures. Total of 679pp. 8⅛ × 11. 22800-2, 22801-0 Pa., Two-vol. set $26.90

THE MARVELOUS LAND OF OZ, L. Frank Baum. Second Oz book, the Scarecrow and Tin Woodman are back with hero named Tip, Oz magic. 136 illustrations. 287pp. 5⅜ × 8½. 20692-0 Pa. $5.95

WILD FOWL DECOYS, Joel Barber. Basic book on the subject, by foremost authority and collector. Reveals history of decoy making and rigging, place in American culture, different kinds of decoys, how to make them, and how to use them. 140 plates. 156pp. 7⅞ × 10¾. 20011-6 Pa. $14.95

HISTORY OF LACE, Mrs. Bury Palliser. Definitive, profusely illustrated chronicle of lace from earliest times to late 19th century. Laces of Italy, Greece, England, France, Belgium, etc. Landmark of needlework scholarship. 266 illustrations. 672pp. 6⅛ × 9¼. 24742-2 Pa. $16.95

ILLUSTRATED GUIDE TO SHAKER FURNITURE, Robert Meader. All furniture and appurtenances, with much on unknown local styles. 235 photos. 146pp. 9 × 12.   22819-3 Pa. $9.95

WHALE SHIPS AND WHALING: A Pictorial Survey, George Francis Dow. Over 200 vintage engravings, drawings, photographs of barks, brigs, cutters, other vessels. Also harpoons, lances, whaling guns, many other artifacts. Comprehensive text by foremost authority. 207 black-and-white illustrations. 288pp. 6 × 9.
24808-9 Pa. $9.95

THE BERTRAMS, Anthony Trollope. Powerful portrayal of blind self-will and thwarted ambition includes one of Trollope's most heartrending love stories. 497pp. 5⅜ × 8½.   25119-5 Pa. $9.95

ADVENTURES WITH A HAND LENS, Richard Headstrom. Clearly written guide to observing and studying flowers and grasses, fish scales, moth and insect wings, egg cases, buds, feathers, seeds, leaf scars, moss, molds, ferns, common crystals, etc.—all with an ordinary, inexpensive magnifying glass. 209 exact line drawings aid in your discoveries. 220pp. 5⅜ × 8½.   23330-8 Pa. $5.95

RODIN ON ART AND ARTISTS, Auguste Rodin. Great sculptor's candid, wide-ranging comments on meaning of art; great artists; relation of sculpture to poetry, painting, music; philosophy of life, more. 76 superb black-and-white illustrations of Rodin's sculpture, drawings and prints. 119pp. 8⅜ × 11¼.   24487-3 Pa. $7.95

FIFTY CLASSIC FRENCH FILMS, 1912–1982: A Pictorial Record, Anthony Slide. Memorable stills from Grand Illusion, Beauty and the Beast, Hiroshima, Mon Amour, many more. Credits, plot synopses, reviews, etc. 160pp. 8¼ × 11.
25256-6 Pa. $11.95

THE PRINCIPLES OF PSYCHOLOGY, William James. Famous long course complete, unabridged. Stream of thought, time perception, memory, experimental methods; great work decades ahead of its time. 94 figures. 1,391pp. 5⅜ × 8½.
20381-6, 20382-4 Pa., Two-vol. set $25.90

BODIES IN A BOOKSHOP, R. T. Campbell. Challenging mystery of blackmail and murder with ingenious plot and superbly drawn characters. In the best tradition of British suspense fiction. 192pp. 5⅜ × 8½.   24720-1 Pa. $5.95

CALLAS: Portrait of a Prima Donna, George Jellinek. Renowned commentator on the musical scene chronicles incredible career and life of the most controversial, fascinating, influential operatic personality of our time. 64 black-and-white photographs. 416pp. 5⅜ × 8¼.   25047-4 Pa. $8.95

GEOMETRY, RELATIVITY AND THE FOURTH DIMENSION, Rudolph Rucker. Exposition of fourth dimension, concepts of relativity as Flatland characters continue adventures. Popular, easily followed yet accurate, profound. 141 illustrations. 133pp. 5⅜ × 8½.   23400-2 Pa. $4.95

HOUSEHOLD STORIES BY THE BROTHERS GRIMM, with pictures by Walter Crane. 53 classic stories—Rumpelstiltskin, Rapunzel, Hansel and Gretel, the Fisherman and his Wife, Snow White, Tom Thumb, Sleeping Beauty, Cinderella, and so much more—lavishly illustrated with original 19th-century drawings. 114 illustrations. x + 269pp. 5⅜ × 8½.   21080-4 Pa. $4.95

SUNDIALS, Albert Waugh. Far and away the best, most thorough coverage of ideas, mathematics concerned, types, construction, adjusting anywhere. Over 100 illustrations. 230pp. 5⅜ × 8½. 22947-5 Pa. $5.95

PICTURE HISTORY OF THE NORMANDIE: With 190 Illustrations, Frank O. Braynard. Full story of legendary French ocean liner: Art Deco interiors, design innovations, furnishings, celebrities, maiden voyage, tragic fire, much more. Extensive text. 144pp. 8⅞ × 11¾. 25257-4 Pa. $11.95

THE FIRST AMERICAN COOKBOOK: A Facsimile of "American Cookery," 1796, Amelia Simmons. Facsimile of the first American-written cookbook published in the United States contains authentic recipes for colonial favorites—pumpkin pudding, winter squash pudding, spruce beer, Indian slapjacks, and more. Introductory Essay and Glossary of colonial cooking terms. 80pp. 5⅜ × 8½. 24710-4 Pa. $3.50

101 PUZZLES IN THOUGHT AND LOGIC, C. R. Wylie, Jr. Solve murders and robberies, find out which fishermen are liars, how a blind man could possibly identify a color—purely by your own reasoning! 107pp. 5⅜ × 8½. 20367-0 Pa. $2.95

ANCIENT EGYPTIAN MYTHS AND LEGENDS, Lewis Spence. Examines animism, totemism, fetishism, creation myths, deities, alchemy, art and magic, other topics. Over 50 illustrations. 432pp. 5⅜ × 8½. 26525-0 Pa. $8.95

ANTHROPOLOGY AND MODERN LIFE, Franz Boas. Great anthropologist's classic treatise on race and culture. Introduction by Ruth Bunzel. Only inexpensive paperback edition. 255pp. 5⅜ × 8½. 25245-0 Pa. $7.95

THE TALE OF PETER RABBIT, Beatrix Potter. The inimitable Peter's terrifying adventure in Mr. McGregor's garden, with all 27 wonderful, full-color Potter illustrations. 55pp. 4¼ × 5½. 22827-4 Pa. $1.75

THREE PROPHETIC SCIENCE FICTION NOVELS, H. G. Wells. *When the Sleeper Wakes, A Story of the Days to Come* and *The Time Machine* (full version). 335pp. 5⅜ × 8½. (Available in U.S. only) 20605-X Pa. $8.95

APICIUS COOKERY AND DINING IN IMPERIAL ROME, edited and translated by Joseph Dommers Vehling. Oldest known cookbook in existence offers readers a clear picture of what foods Romans ate, how they prepared them, etc. 49 illustrations. 301pp. 6⅛ × 9¼. 23563-7 Pa. $8.95

SHAKESPEARE LEXICON AND QUOTATION DICTIONARY, Alexander Schmidt. Full definitions, locations, shades of meaning of every word in plays and poems. More than 50,000 exact quotations. 1,485pp. 6½ × 9¼.
22726-X, 22727-8 Pa., Two-vol. set $31.90

THE WORLD'S GREAT SPEECHES, edited by Lewis Copeland and Lawrence W. Lamm. Vast collection of 278 speeches from Greeks to 1970. Powerful and effective models; unique look at history. 842pp. 5⅜ × 8½. 20468-5 Pa. $12.95

PLANTS OF THE BIBLE, Harold N. Moldenke and Alma L. Moldenke. Standard reference to all 230 plants mentioned in Scriptures. Latin name, biblical reference, uses, modern identity, much more. Unsurpassed encyclopedic resource for scholars, botanists, nature lovers, students of Bible. Bibliography. Indexes. 123 black-and-white illustrations. 384pp. 6 × 9. 25069-5 Pa. $9.95

FAMOUS AMERICAN WOMEN: A Biographical Dictionary from Colonial Times to the Present, Robert McHenry, ed. From Pocahontas to Rosa Parks, 1,035 distinguished American women documented in separate biographical entries. Accurate, up-to-date data, numerous categories, spans 400 years. Indices. 493pp. 6½ × 9¼. 24523-3 Pa. $11.95

THE FABULOUS INTERIORS OF THE GREAT OCEAN LINERS IN HISTORIC PHOTOGRAPHS, William H. Miller, Jr. Some 200 superb photographs capture exquisite interiors of world's great "floating palaces"—1890s to 1980s: *Titanic, Ile de France, Queen Elizabeth, United States, Europa,* more. Approx. 200 black-and-white photographs. Captions. Text. Introduction. 160pp. 8⅞ × 11¾. 24756-2 Pa. $10.95

THE GREAT LUXURY LINERS, 1927–1954: A Photographic Record, William H. Miller, Jr. Nostalgic tribute to heyday of ocean liners. 186 photos of *Ile de France, Normandie, Leviathan, Queen Elizabeth, United States,* many others. Interior and exterior views. Introduction. Captions. 160pp. 9 × 12. 24056-8 Pa. $12.95

A NATURAL HISTORY OF THE DUCKS, John Charles Phillips. Great landmark of ornithology offers complete detailed coverage of nearly 200 species and subspecies of ducks: gadwall, sheldrake, merganser, pintail, many more. 74 full-color plates, 102 black-and-white. Bibliography. Total of 1,920pp. 8⅝ × 11¼. 25141-1, 25142-X Cloth., Two-vol. set $100.00

THE COMPLETE "MASTERS OF THE POSTER": All 256 Color Plates from "Les Maîtres de l'Affiche", Stanley Appelbaum (ed.). The most famous compilation ever made of the art of the great age of the poster, featuring works by Chéret, Steinlen, Toulouse-Lautrec, nearly 100 other artists. One poster per page. 272pp. 9¼ × 12¼. 26309-6 Pa. $29.95

THE TEN BOOKS OF ARCHITECTURE: The 1755 Leoni Edition, Leon Battista Alberti. Rare classic helped introduce the glories of ancient architecture to the Renaissance. 68 black-and-white plates. 336pp. 8⅜ × 11¼. 25239-6 Pa. $14.95

MISS MACKENZIE, Anthony Trollope. Minor masterpieces by Victorian master unmasks many truths about life in 19th-century England. First inexpensive edition in years. 392pp. 5⅜ × 8½. 25201-9 Pa. $8.95

THE RIME OF THE ANCIENT MARINER, Gustave Doré, Samuel Taylor Coleridge. Dramatic engravings considered by many to be his greatest work. The terrifying space of the open sea, the storms and whirlpools of an unknown ocean, the ice of Antarctica, more—all rendered in a powerful, chilling manner. Full text. 38 plates. 77pp. 9¼ × 12. 22305-1 Pa. $4.95

THE EXPEDITIONS OF ZEBULON MONTGOMERY PIKE, Zebulon Montgomery Pike. Fascinating firsthand accounts (1805–6) of exploration of Mississippi River, Indian wars, capture by Spanish dragoons, much more. 1,088pp. 5⅜ × 8½. 25254-X, 25255-8 Pa., Two-vol. set $25.90

A CONCISE HISTORY OF PHOTOGRAPHY: Third Revised Edition, Helmut Gernsheim. Best one-volume history—camera obscura, photochemistry, daguerreotypes, evolution of cameras, film, more. Also artistic aspects—landscape, portraits, fine art, etc. 281 black-and-white photographs. 26 in color. 176pp. 8⅜ × 11¼.
25128-4 Pa. $14.95

THE DORÉ BIBLE ILLUSTRATIONS, Gustave Doré. 241 detailed plates from the Bible: the Creation scenes, Adam and Eve, Flood, Babylon, battle sequences, life of Jesus, etc. Each plate is accompanied by the verses from the King James version of the Bible. 241pp. 9 × 12. 23004-X Pa. $9.95

WANDERINGS IN WEST AFRICA, Richard F. Burton. Great Victorian scholar/adventurer's invaluable descriptions of African tribal rituals, fetishism, culture, art, much more. Fascinating 19th-century account. 624pp. 5⅜ × 8½. 26890-X Pa. $12.95

HISTORIC HOMES OF THE AMERICAN PRESIDENTS, Second Revised Edition, Irvin Haas. Guide to homes occupied by every president from Washington to Bush. Visiting hours, travel routes, more. 175 photos. 160pp. 8¼ × 11.
26751-2 Pa. $9.95

THE HISTORY OF THE LEWIS AND CLARK EXPEDITION, Meriwether Lewis and William Clark, edited by Elliott Coues. Classic edition of Lewis and Clark's day-by-day journals that later became the basis for U.S. claims to Oregon and the West. Accurate and invaluable geographical, botanical, biological, meteorological and anthropological material. Total of 1,508pp. 5⅜ × 8½.
21268-8, 21269-6, 21270-X Pa., Three-vol. set $29.85

LANGUAGE, TRUTH AND LOGIC, Alfred J. Ayer. Famous, clear introduction to Vienna, Cambridge schools of Logical Positivism. Role of philosophy, elimination of metaphysics, nature of analysis, etc. 160pp. 5⅜ × 8½. (Available in U.S. and Canada only) 20010-8 Pa. $3.95

MATHEMATICS FOR THE NONMATHEMATICIAN, Morris Kline. Detailed, college-level treatment of mathematics in cultural and historical context, with numerous exercises. For liberal arts students. Preface. Recommended Reading Lists. Tables. Index. Numerous black-and-white figures. xvi + 641pp. 5⅜ × 8½.
24823-2 Pa. $11.95

HANDBOOK OF PICTORIAL SYMBOLS, Rudolph Modley. 3,250 signs and symbols, many systems in full; official or heavy commercial use. Arranged by subject. Most in Pictorial Archive series. 143pp. 8⅛ × 11. 23357-X Pa. $8.95

INCIDENTS OF TRAVEL IN YUCATAN, John L. Stephens. Classic (1843) exploration of jungles of Yucatan, looking for evidences of Maya civilization. Travel adventures, Mexican and Indian culture, etc. Total of 669pp. 5⅜ × 8½.
20926-1, 20927-X Pa., Two-vol. set $13.90

CATALOG OF DOVER BOOKS

DEGAS: An Intimate Portrait, Ambroise Vollard. Charming, anecdotal memoir by famous art dealer of one of the greatest 19th-century French painters. 14 black-and-white illustrations. Introduction by Harold L. Van Doren. 96pp. 5⅜ × 8½.
25131-4 Pa. $4.95

PERSONAL NARRATIVE OF A PILGRIMAGE TO AL-MADINAH AND MECCAH, Richard F. Burton. Great travel classic by remarkably colorful personality. Burton, disguised as a Moroccan, visited sacred shrines of Islam, narrowly escaping death. 47 illustrations. 959pp. 5⅜ × 8½.
21217-3, 21218-1 Pa., Two-vol. set $19.90

PHRASE AND WORD ORIGINS, A. H. Holt. Entertaining, reliable, modern study of more than 1,200 colorful words, phrases, origins and histories. Much unexpected information. 254pp. 5⅜ × 8½.
20758-7 Pa. $5.95

THE RED THUMB MARK, R. Austin Freeman. In this first Dr. Thorndyke case, the great scientific detective draws fascinating conclusions from the nature of a single fingerprint. Exciting story, authentic science. 320pp. 5⅜ × 8½. (Available in U.S. only)
25210-8 Pa. $6.95

AN EGYPTIAN HIEROGLYPHIC DICTIONARY, E. A. Wallis Budge. Monumental work containing about 25,000 words or terms that occur in texts ranging from 3000 B.C. to 600 A.D. Each entry consists of a transliteration of the word, the word in hieroglyphs, and the meaning in English. 1,314pp. 6⅜ × 10.
23615-3, 23616-1 Pa., Two-vol. set $35.90

THE COMPLEAT STRATEGYST: Being a Primer on the Theory of Games of Strategy, J. D. Williams. Highly entertaining classic describes, with many illustrated examples, how to select best strategies in conflict situations. Prefaces. Appendices. xvi + 268pp. 5⅜ × 8½.
25101-2 Pa. $7.95

THE ROAD TO OZ, L. Frank Baum. Dorothy meets the Shaggy Man, little Button-Bright and the Rainbow's beautiful daughter in this delightful trip to the magical Land of Oz. 272pp. 5⅜ × 8.
25208-6 Pa. $5.95

POINT AND LINE TO PLANE, Wassily Kandinsky. Seminal exposition of role of point, line, other elements in nonobjective painting. Essential to understanding 20th-century art. 127 illustrations. 192pp. 6½ × 9¼.
23808-3 Pa. $5.95

LADY ANNA, Anthony Trollope. Moving chronicle of Countess Lovel's bitter struggle to win for herself and daughter Anna their rightful rank and fortune—perhaps at cost of sanity itself. 384pp. 5⅜ × 8½.
24669-8 Pa. $8.95

EGYPTIAN MAGIC, E. A. Wallis Budge. Sums up all that is known about magic in Ancient Egypt: the role of magic in controlling the gods, powerful amulets that warded off evil spirits, scarabs of immortality, use of wax images, formulas and spells, the secret name, much more. 253pp. 5⅜ × 8½.
22681-6 Pa. $4.95

THE DANCE OF SIVA, Ananda Coomaraswamy. Preeminent authority unfolds the vast metaphysic of India: the revelation of her art, conception of the universe, social organization, etc. 27 reproductions of art masterpieces. 192pp. 5⅜ × 8½.
24817-8 Pa. $6.95

CHRISTMAS CUSTOMS AND TRADITIONS, Clement A. Miles. Origin, evolution, significance of religious, secular practices. Caroling, gifts, yule logs, much more. Full, scholarly yet fascinating; non-sectarian. 400pp. 5⅜ × 8½.
23354-5 Pa. $7.95

THE HUMAN FIGURE IN MOTION, Eadweard Muybridge. More than 4,500 stopped-action photos, in action series, showing undraped men, women, children jumping, lying down, throwing, sitting, wrestling, carrying, etc. 390pp. 7⅞ × 10⅝.
20204-6 Cloth. $24.95

THE MAN WHO WAS THURSDAY, Gilbert Keith Chesterton. Witty, fast-paced novel about a club of anarchists in turn-of-the-century London. Brilliant social, religious, philosophical speculations. 128pp. 5⅜ × 8½. 25121-7 Pa. $3.95

A CÉZANNE SKETCHBOOK: Figures, Portraits, Landscapes and Still Lifes, Paul Cézanne. Great artist experiments with tonal effects, light, mass, other qualities in over 100 drawings. A revealing view of developing master painter, precursor of Cubism. 102 black-and-white illustrations. 144pp. 8¾ × 6⅜. 24790-2 Pa. $6.95

AN ENCYCLOPEDIA OF BATTLES: Accounts of Over 1,560 Battles from 1479 B.C. to the Present, David Eggenberger. Presents essential details of every major battle in recorded history, from the first battle of Megiddo in 1479 B.C. to Grenada in 1984. List of Battle Maps. New Appendix covering the years 1967–1984. Index. 99 illustrations. 544pp. 6½ × 9¼. 24913-1 Pa. $14.95

AN ETYMOLOGICAL DICTIONARY OF MODERN ENGLISH, Ernest Weekley. Richest, fullest work, by foremost British lexicographer. Detailed word histories. Inexhaustible. Total of 856pp. 6½ × 9¼.
21873-2, 21874-0 Pa., Two-vol. set $19.90

WEBSTER'S AMERICAN MILITARY BIOGRAPHIES, edited by Robert McHenry. Over 1,000 figures who shaped 3 centuries of American military history. Detailed biographies of Nathan Hale, Douglas MacArthur, Mary Hallaren, others. Chronologies of engagements, more. Introduction. Addenda. 1,033 entries in alphabetical order. xi + 548pp. 6½ × 9¼. (Available in U.S. only)
24758-9 Pa. $13.95

LIFE IN ANCIENT EGYPT, Adolf Erman. Detailed older account, with much not in more recent books: domestic life, religion, magic, medicine, commerce, and whatever else needed for complete picture. Many illustrations. 597pp. 5⅜ × 8½.
22632-8 Pa. $9.95

HISTORIC COSTUME IN PICTURES, Braun & Schneider. Over 1,450 costumed figures shown, covering a wide variety of peoples: kings, emperors, nobles, priests, servants, soldiers, scholars, townsfolk, peasants, merchants, courtiers, cavaliers, and more. 256pp. 8⅜ × 11¼. 23150-X Pa. $9.95

THE NOTEBOOKS OF LEONARDO DA VINCI, edited by J. P. Richter. Extracts from manuscripts reveal great genius; on painting, sculpture, anatomy, sciences, geography, etc. Both Italian and English. 186 ms. pages reproduced, plus 500 additional drawings, including studies for *Last Supper, Sforza* monument, etc. 860pp. 7⅞ × 10¾. 22572-0, 22573-9 Pa., Two-vol. set $35.90

CATALOG OF DOVER BOOKS

THE ART NOUVEAU STYLE BOOK OF ALPHONSE MUCHA: All 72 Plates from "Documents Decoratifs" in Original Color, Alphonse Mucha. Rare copyright-free design portfolio by high priest of Art Nouveau. Jewelry, wallpaper, stained glass, furniture, figure studies, plant and animal motifs, etc. Only complete one-volume edition. 80pp. 9⅜ × 12¼. 24044-4 Pa. $10.95

ANIMALS: 1,419 Copyright-Free Illustrations of Mammals, Birds, Fish, Insects, Etc., edited by Jim Harter. Clear wood engravings present, in extremely lifelike poses, over 1,000 species of animals. One of the most extensive pictorial sourcebooks of its kind. Captions. Index. 284pp. 9 × 12. 23766-4 Pa. $10.95

OBELISTS FLY HIGH, C. Daly King. Masterpiece of American detective fiction, long out of print, involves murder on a 1935 transcontinental flight—"a very thrilling story"—NY Times. Unabridged and unaltered republication of the edition published by William Collins Sons & Co. Ltd., London, 1935. 288pp. 5⅜ × 8½. (Available in U.S. only) 25036-9 Pa. $5.95

VICTORIAN AND EDWARDIAN FASHION: A Photographic Survey, Alison Gernsheim. First fashion history completely illustrated by contemporary photographs. Full text plus 235 photos, 1840–1914, in which many celebrities appear. 240pp. 6½ × 9¼. 24205-6 Pa. $8.95

THE ART OF THE FRENCH ILLUSTRATED BOOK, 1700–1914, Gordon N. Ray. Over 630 superb book illustrations by Fragonard, Delacroix, Daumier, Doré, Grandville, Manet, Mucha, Steinlen, Toulouse-Lautrec and many others. Preface. Introduction. 633 halftones. Indices of artists, authors & titles, binders and provenances. Appendices. Bibliography. 608pp. 8⅜ × 11¼. 25086-5 Pa. $24.95

THE WONDERFUL WIZARD OF OZ, L. Frank Baum. Facsimile in full color of America's finest children's classic. 143 illustrations by W. W. Denslow. 267pp. 5⅜ × 8½. 20691-2 Pa. $7.95

FOLLOWING THE EQUATOR: A Journey Around the World, Mark Twain. Great writer's 1897 account of circumnavigating the globe by steamship. Ironic humor, keen observations, vivid and fascinating descriptions of exotic places. 197 illustrations. 720pp. 5⅜ × 8½. 26113-1 Pa. $15.95

THE FRIENDLY STARS, Martha Evans Martin & Donald Howard Menzel. Classic text marshalls the stars together in an engaging, nontechnical survey, presenting them as sources of beauty in night sky. 23 illustrations. Foreword. 2 star charts. Index. 147pp. 5⅜ × 8½. 21099-5 Pa. $3.95

FADS AND FALLACIES IN THE NAME OF SCIENCE, Martin Gardner. Fair, witty appraisal of cranks, quacks, and quackeries of science and pseudoscience: hollow earth, Velikovsky, orgone energy, Dianetics, flying saucers, Bridey Murphy, food and medical fads, etc. Revised, expanded In the Name of Science. "A very able and even-tempered presentation."—The New Yorker. 363pp. 5⅜ × 8. 20394-8 Pa. $6.95

ANCIENT EGYPT: Its Culture and History, J. E. Manchip White. From predynastics through Ptolemies: society, history, political structure, religion, daily life, literature, cultural heritage. 48 plates. 217pp. 5⅜ × 8½. 22548-8 Pa. $5.95

SIR HARRY HOTSPUR OF HUMBLETHWAITE, Anthony Trollope. Incisive, unconventional psychological study of a conflict between a wealthy baronet, his idealistic daughter, and their scapegrace cousin. The 1870 novel in its first inexpensive edition in years. 250pp. 5⅜ × 8½. 24953-0 Pa. $6.95

LASERS AND HOLOGRAPHY, Winston E. Kock. Sound introduction to burgeoning field, expanded (1981) for second edition. Wave patterns, coherence, lasers, diffraction, zone plates, properties of holograms, recent advances. 84 illustrations. 160pp. 5⅜ × 8¼. (Except in United Kingdom) 24041-X Pa. $4.95

INTRODUCTION TO ARTIFICIAL INTELLIGENCE: Second, Enlarged Edition, Philip C. Jackson, Jr. Comprehensive survey of artificial intelligence—the study of how machines (computers) can be made to act intelligently. Includes introductory and advanced material. Extensive notes updating the main text. 132 black-and-white illustrations. 512pp. 5⅜ × 8½. 24864-X Pa. $10.95

HISTORY OF INDIAN AND INDONESIAN ART, Ananda K. Coomaraswamy. Over 400 illustrations illuminate classic study of Indian art from earliest Harappa finds to early 20th century. Provides philosophical, religious and social insights. 304pp. 6⅜ × 9⅜. 25005-9 Pa. $11.95

THE GOLEM, Gustav Meyrink. Most famous supernatural novel in modern European literature, set in Ghetto of Old Prague around 1890. Compelling story of mystical experiences, strange transformations, profound terror. 13 black-and-white illustrations. 224pp. 5⅜ × 8½. 25025-3 Pa. $7.95

PICTORIAL ENCYCLOPEDIA OF HISTORIC ARCHITECTURAL PLANS, DETAILS AND ELEMENTS: With 1,880 Line Drawings of Arches, Domes, Doorways, Facades, Gables, Windows, etc., John Theodore Haneman. Sourcebook of inspiration for architects, designers, others. Bibliography. Captions. 141pp. 9 × 12. 24605-1 Pa. $8.95

BENCHLEY LOST AND FOUND, Robert Benchley. Finest humor from early 30s, about pet peeves, child psychologists, post office and others. Mostly unavailable elsewhere. 73 illustrations by Peter Arno and others. 183pp. 5⅜ × 8½. 22410-4 Pa. $4.95

ERTÉ GRAPHICS, Erté. Collection of striking color graphics: *Seasons, Alphabet, Numerals, Aces* and *Precious Stones.* 50 plates, including 4 on covers. 48pp. 9⅜ × 12¼. 23580-7 Pa. $7.95

THE JOURNAL OF HENRY D. THOREAU, edited by Bradford Torrey, F. H. Allen. Complete reprinting of 14 volumes, 1837–61, over two million words; the sourcebooks for *Walden,* etc. Definitive. All original sketches, plus 75 photographs. 1,804pp. 8½ × 12¼. 20312-3, 20313-1 Cloth., Two-vol. set $130.00

CASTLES: Their Construction and History, Sidney Toy. Traces castle development from ancient roots. Nearly 200 photographs and drawings illustrate moats, keeps, baileys, many other features. Caernarvon, Dover Castles, Hadrian's Wall, Tower of London, dozens more. 256pp. 5⅜ × 8¼. 24898-4 Pa. $7.95

AMERICAN CLIPPER SHIPS: 1833–1858, Octavius T. Howe & Frederick C. Matthews. Fully-illustrated, encyclopedic review of 352 clipper ships from the period of America's greatest maritime supremacy. Introduction. 109 halftones. 5 black-and-white line illustrations. Index. Total of 928pp. 5⅜ × 8½.
25115-2, 25116-0 Pa., Two-vol. set $21.90

TOWARDS A NEW ARCHITECTURE, Le Corbusier. Pioneering manifesto by great architect, near legendary founder of "International School." Technical and aesthetic theories, views on industry, economics, relation of form to function, "mass-production spirit," much more. Profusely illustrated. Unabridged translation of 13th French edition. Introduction by Frederick Etchells. 320pp. 6⅛ × 9¼. (Available in U.S. only)
25023-7 Pa. $8.95

THE BOOK OF KELLS, edited by Blanche Cirker. Inexpensive collection of 32 full-color, full-page plates from the greatest illuminated manuscript of the Middle Ages, painstakingly reproduced from rare facsimile edition. Publisher's Note. Captions. 32pp. 9⅜ × 12¼. (Available in U.S. only)
24345-1 Pa. $5.95

BEST SCIENCE FICTION STORIES OF H. G. WELLS, H. G. Wells. Full novel *The Invisible Man*, plus 17 short stories: "The Crystal Egg," "Aepyornis Island," "The Strange Orchid," etc. 303pp. 5⅜ × 8½. (Available in U.S. only)
21531-8 Pa. $6.95

AMERICAN SAILING SHIPS: Their Plans and History, Charles G. Davis. Photos, construction details of schooners, frigates, clippers, other sailcraft of 18th to early 20th centuries—plus entertaining discourse on design, rigging, nautical lore, much more. 137 black-and-white illustrations. 240pp. 6⅛ × 9¼.
24658-2 Pa. $6.95

ENTERTAINING MATHEMATICAL PUZZLES, Martin Gardner. Selection of author's favorite conundrums involving arithmetic, money, speed, etc., with lively commentary. Complete solutions. 112pp. 5⅜ × 8½. 25211-6 Pa. $3.95

THE WILL TO BELIEVE, HUMAN IMMORTALITY, William James. Two books bound together. Effect of irrational on logical, and arguments for human immortality. 402pp. 5⅜ × 8½. 20291-7 Pa. $8.95

THE HAUNTED MONASTERY and THE CHINESE MAZE MURDERS, Robert Van Gulik. 2 full novels by Van Gulik continue adventures of Judge Dee and his companions. An evil Taoist monastery, seemingly supernatural events; overgrown topiary maze that hides strange crimes. Set in 7th-century China. 27 illustrations. 328pp. 5⅜ × 8½. 23502-5 Pa. $6.95

CELEBRATED CASES OF JUDGE DEE (DEE GOONG AN), translated by Robert Van Gulik. Authentic 18th-century Chinese detective novel; Dee and associates solve three interlocked cases. Led to Van Gulik's own stories with same characters. Extensive introduction. 9 illustrations. 237pp. 5⅜ × 8½.
23337-5 Pa. $5.95

Prices subject to change without notice.

Available at your book dealer or write for free catalog to Dept. GI, Dover Publications, Inc., 31 East 2nd St., Mineola, N.Y. 11501. Dover publishes more than 400 books each year on science, elementary and advanced mathematics, biology, music, art, literary history, social sciences and other areas.